PREFACE

1. Scope

This publication provides doctrine for the planning, execution, and assessment of airspace control during joint operations across the full range of military operations. It also discusses airspace control across the phases of military operations, emphasizing transitions from, and back to, civilian controlled airspace.

2. Purpose

This publication has been prepared under the direction of the Chairman of the Joint Chiefs of Staff (CJCS). It sets forth doctrine to govern the joint activities and performance of the Armed Forces of the United States in joint operations and provides the doctrinal basis for interagency coordination and US military involvement in multinational operations. It provides military guidance for the exercise of authority by combatant commanders and other joint force commanders (JFCs) and prescribes doctrine for joint operations and training. It provides military guidance for use by the Armed Forces in preparing their appropriate plans. It is not the intent of this publication to restrict the authority of the JFC from organizing the force and executing the mission in a manner the JFC deems most appropriate to ensure unity of effort in the accomplishment of the overall mission.

3. Application

a. Doctrine and guidance established in this publication apply to the commanders of combatant commands, subunified commands, joint task forces, and subordinate components of these commands. These principles and guidance also may apply when significant forces of one Service are attached to forces of another Service or when significant forces of one Service support forces of another Service.

b. The guidance in this publication is authoritative; as such, this doctrine will be followed except when, in the judgment of the commander, exceptional circumstances dictate otherwise. If conflicts arise between the contents of this publication and the contents of Service publications, this publication will take precedence for the activities of joint forces unless the CJCS, normally in coordination with the other members of the Joint Chiefs of Staff, has provided more current and specific guidance. Commanders of forces operating as part of a multinational (alliance or coalition) military command should follow multinational doctrine and procedures ratified by the United States. For doctrine and procedures not ratified by the United States, commanders should evaluate and follow the multinational command's doctrine and procedures, where applicable and consistent with US law, regulations, and doctrine.

For the Chairman of the Joint Chiefs of Staff:

LLOYD J. AUSTIN III
Lieutenant General, USA
Director, Joint Staff

- **Changes title from** *Joint Doctrine for Airspace Control in the Combat Zone* **to** *Joint Airspace Control*

- **Replaces unmanned aerial vehicle with unmanned aircraft and adds use of term unmanned aircraft system**

- Expands the basic principles of airspace control to include centralized airspace planning and for having **trained joint airspace users and joint airspace control system personnel to work complex airspace**

- Addresses airspace control with regard to differing priorities between civil and military airspace procedures

- Incorporates paragraph to address airspace control risk considerations

- Gives explanation of the joint air tasking cycle

- Expands the discussion on methods of airspace control

- Adds chapter to address airspace execution in the various phases of a joint operation

- Updates figure listing and describing/defining **airspace coordinating and fire support coordination measures**

- **Deletes airspace control order development appendix**

- Modifies the definitions for airspace control, coordinating altitude, fighter engagement zone, high-altitude missile engagement zone, joint air operations plan, joint engagement zone, low-altitude missile engagement zone, low-level-transit route, and weapons engagement zone.

- **Removes the terms and definitions from Joint Publication 1-02, Department of Defense Dictionary of Military and Associated Terms, for aircraft control and warning system, aircraft vectoring, airport surveillance radar, airport traffic control, airspace control boundary, airspace control center, airspace control facility, airspace control in the combat zone, airspace restrictions, air space warning area, air traffic control and landing system, air traffic control center, air traffic controller, air traffic identification, combined operations, and unmanned aerial vehicle**

Intentionally Blank

TABLE OF CONTENTS

CHAPTER IV
AIRSPACE CONTROL EXECUTION BY PHASE

APPENDIX

GLOSSARY

FIGURE

- **Prescribes doctrine for joint airspace control in the joint operational area**

- **Discusses the organization and coordination for and the broad duties central to effective airspace control**

- **Sets out the principles for airspace control planning to include phasing considerations**

- **Details requirements for effective airspace control execution by operational phase**

Overview

General.

This joint publication prescribes doctrine for joint airspace control in the operational area. The prescribed doctrine is broadly stated to fit a wide range of situations requiring military control of airspace. It outlines fundamental principles, relationships, and broad operational-level guidelines, and is intended to provide the basic framework upon which to build an airspace control system (ACS) for an operational area.

Command and Control.

The joint force commander (JFC) normally designates a joint force air component commander (JFACC) as commander for joint air operations. The JFC also normally designates an area air defense commander (AADC) and an airspace control authority (ACA). When the JFC designates a JFACC, the JFC also normally designates the JFACC as the AADC and ACA. The ACA plans, coordinates, and develops airspace control procedures and operates the ACS. The JFC may designate a separate ACA and/or AADC, in which case, close coordination is essential for unity of effort.

Airspace Control Plan (ACP).

The ACA develops a specific airspace control plan (ACP) that is approved by the JFC. The ACP should be closely integrated with the JFC-approved area air defense plan (AADP) developed by the AADC.

Joint Airspace Control.

Joint airspace control increases combat effectiveness by promoting the safe, efficient, and flexible use of airspace with minimum restraint upon airspace users, and includes coordinating, integrating, and regulating airspace to increase operational effectiveness. Effective airspace control reduces the risk of fratricide, enhances air defense, and permits flexibility. Airspace control operations may begin prior to (and continue after) combat operations and may transition through degrees of civil and military authority. The JFC defines the relationship between the ACA and component commanders. Airspace control is essential to operational effectiveness in accomplishing JFC objectives across the range of military operations.

Basic Principles.

Airspace is a crucial part of the operational environment used by all components. A high concentration of friendly surface, subsurface, and air-launched weapon systems must share this airspace without unnecessarily hindering the application of combat power. The primary goal of airspace control is to enhance effectiveness of the joint force and increase the safety of joint air operations. Basic principles include:

- Support unity of effort.
- Reduce the risk of fratricide and increase the effectiveness of air defense.
- Centralized airspace planning and decentralized execution.
- Close liaison and coordination among all airspace users.
- Airspace control procedures provide flexibility through a combination of positive and procedural control measures.
- A reliable, integrated, jam-resistant, and secure communications network for the ACS.
- Survivable and redundant air control assets.
- The structure of the ACS is responsive to developing threats and the unfolding operation.
- Airspace control functions rely on airspace management resources, but these functions are separate and distinct from air traffic control (ATC), which is nevertheless interoperable with and integral to the ACS.
- Flexibility and simplicity are emphasized.

- ACSs should be interoperable and integrated.
- Support 24-hour operations in all weather and environmental conditions.
- Provide appropriate training for joint airspace users and joint ACS personnel.

Organization and Coordination

Organization.

The following broad duties are central to effective airspace control:

- The JFC is responsible for airspace control in the joint operations area (JOA).
- The JFACC plans, coordinates, and monitors joint air operations and allocates and tasks joint air operations forces based on the JFC's concept of operations (CONOPS) and air apportionment decision, and is normally designated as both AADC and ACA.
- Component commanders advise the JFC on employment, direction and control of component forces, and each plans and executes a portion of the total air effort and interacts with other components.
- The ACA develops airspace control policies and procedures for all airspace users and establishes an ACS that coordinates and integrates airspace use under JFC authority.
- The AADC is responsible for defensive counterair (DCA) operations, which include both air and missile threats.

Liaison Requirements.

Liaison requirements vary based on the mission, size of the force, and various operation and mission variables; identification of liaison requirements is a key planning and command and control (C2) consideration.

ACP.

The ACP establishes general guidance and procedures for the ACS in the operational area and is approved by the JFC. The ACP and AADP are integrated with the JFC's operation plan and orders, and considers procedures and interfaces with international or regional air traffic systems. The ACP should be preplanned, to the degree possible, in a simplified, understandable format. Because the airspace control area normally coincides with air defense boundaries, coordination between airspace control and area air defense operations is essential.

Airspace Control Order (ACO).

The airspace control order (ACO) implements specific control procedures for established time periods, and is an order published either as part of the air tasking order (ATO) or as a separate document. It defines and establishes airspace for military operations as coordinated by the ACA, and notifies all agencies of the effective time of activation and the structure of the airspace. Timely promulgation of ACO changes to all airspace users, to include multinational forces, is essential.

ACO Development.

The JFC may elect to delegate specific authority for airspace control to the component commanders, and may also task component commanders to generate individual ACOs for assigned sectors. The ACA provides continuity along sector boundaries and integration of each sector authority's ACO within the ACP guidelines.

The Joint Air Tasking Cycle.

The joint air tasking process is a systematic cycle that focuses joint air efforts on supporting operational requirements. It provides for effective and efficient employment of joint air capabilities through an iterative, cyclic process for the planning, apportionment, allocation, coordination, tasking, and execution of joint air missions and sorties within the guidance of the JFC. The process accommodates changing tactical situations or JFC guidance as well as requests for support from component commanders. Planners develop airspace control and air defense instructions in sufficient detail to allow components to plan and execute air missions listed in the ATO. The ATO is the operation order or mission assignment for all aircraft missions flown under control of the JFACC in the operational area and shows all missions operating in the operational area during the effective time period. In some theaters, numerous airspace procedures and airspace usages are published in the special instructions (SPINS).

Communications and Security Considerations.

The ACS should be joint, interoperable, survivable, sustainable, redundant, and supported by jam-resistant, secure C2 networks. It should allow users to maintain situational awareness and respond to an evolving enemy situation and friendly air operations. Timely integration of various data networked among authorized airspace control agencies and C2 nodes permits developing a common operational picture. Secure ACSs are crucial to effective airspace control capabilities. Information assurance (IA) programs are methods to protect ACSs and information. IA is essential to airspace control, and considerations for operations security (OPSEC) must be applied. ACSs, especially voice radio communications, are susceptible to frequency jammers, data emitters, or other radio transmitters operating in the same segment of the electromagnetic spectrum. Communications outage procedures should be clearly defined. Airspace management planning and execution must be integrated with spectrum management.

Airspace Control Planning Considerations

Airspace Considerations by Phase.

Phasing provides an orderly schedule of military operations, indicates preplanned shifts in priorities and intent, and is a way to view and conduct a complex joint operation in manageable parts. The main purpose of phasing is to integrate and synchronize related activities. Phasing may be used to modify the prioritization of airspace control missions and priorities for operations. Airspace planners should consider that all operations will not smoothly transition between phases. The phasing construct is a model to start planning efforts, but each conflict is different and may not resemble the model at different points in time. Airspace control and management should be a part of contingency and crisis action planning from the beginning. During joint operations, the likely mix of military and commercial air traffic activity during various phases may make airspace control more complex than during combat.

Airspace Control Risk Considerations.

Risk is a fundamental consideration of airspace control. Each Service and functional component uses the airspace with maximum availability consistent with the JFC's acceptable level of risk for all airspace users (including fires), which should be clearly delineated in the ACP. During all phases the assumption of risk is a command decision.

Planning for Joint Airspace Control.

Each operational area has specific requirements for airspace control. These requirements must be determined as early as possible and incorporated in the overall planning effort. Every joint/multinational force is different, and the forces assigned will have specific operational requirements for airspace. The following broad principles of planning are essential:

- Interoperability
- Mass and timing
- Unity of effort
- Integrated planning cycles
- Degraded operations

Integration of Joint Airspace Control and Civil Air Traffic Control Operations.

Integration of joint airspace control and civil ATC is vital to successful joint/multinational air operations. The ACP should provide procedures to fully integrate the military and civil ATC resources responsible for terminal-area airspace control or en route ATC when required.

Integration of Joint Airspace Control and Air Defense Operations.

Integration of joint airspace control and air defense and the prioritization and integration of joint airspace control and air defense activities are essential. Airspace control procedures assist in aircraft identification, facilitate engagement of enemy aircraft, and provide safe passage of friendly aircraft. Rules of engagement and procedures must give air defense forces freedom to engage hostile aircraft and missiles, but procedures must be established in the ACP and the ACO to allow identification of friendly aircraft, to prevent delays in offensive operations, and reduce the risk of fratricide. These procedures need to be simple to execute and may include visual, electronic, geographic, and/or maneuver means for sorting friend from foe. The procedures should allow coordinated employment of air, land, or maritime air defense systems, and use the inherent flexibility of air defense airborne platforms to mass forces to meet enemy attacks.

Airspace Integration and Joint Fires.

Airspace control procedures increase in complexity and detail when air forces operate in proximity to, or in conjunction with, surface forces. Liaison elements are vital. Each area of operations (AO) may be defined with specific boundaries, and within each AO there are typically maneuver control measures such as boundaries, fire support coordination measures (FSCMs), airspace coordination measures (ACMs), a fire support coordination line (FSCL), or multiples of these measures. Close coordination is required to deconflict and integrate airspace use with the employment of joint fires. Component fire support agencies establish FSCMs. ACMs facilitate the efficient use of airspace to accomplish missions and simultaneously provide safeguards for friendly forces. The airspace coordinating entities should be included in the ACP and promulgated in the ACO.

Methods of Joint Airspace Control.

The methods of airspace control vary across the range of military operations, from positive control of all air assets in an airspace control area to procedural control of all such assets, or any effective combination. ACPs and systems accommodate these methods based on component, joint and national capabilities, and requirements. The airspace control structure must be responsive to evolving enemy threat conditions and changing tactical situations.

Enemy Air Engagement Operations.

Engaging enemy aircraft with friendly air, land, and maritime assets must be fully coordinated to optimize all aspects of friendly combat power. Joint engagement zone (JEZ) operations involve the employment and integration of multiple air defense systems in order to simultaneously engage enemy targets in the operational area. Successful JEZ operations depend on positively identifying friendly, neutral, and enemy aircraft. JEZ operations require effective C2 and positive control is normally used in a JEZ. Fighter engagement zone operations usually occur above and beyond the range of surface-based air defenses, and are highly dependent on coordination and flexibility within the ACS. Missile engagement zone (MEZ) operations are ideal for point defense of critical assets, protection of maneuver units, and area coverage of the joint security area. MEZ operations offer the ability to engage the enemy with a high- and low-altitude, all-weather capability beyond the forward line of own troops (FLOT) or disrupt massed enemy air attacks prior to committing fighter assets, and are effective across the full range of air defense operations and enemy threats. For urgent or emergency combat situations, the ACA can authorize deviations from established policies and procedures. When the circumstances necessitate rapid deployment and employment of forces for which there are no approved plans or previously established ACPs, a temporary ACS responsive to immediate tactical or operational requirements will be established. Airspace control and integration of friendly electronic warfare and suppression of enemy air defenses are integrated into the overall planning effort.

Multinational Integration Issues.

International agreements, enemy and friendly force structures, commanders' CONOPS, and the operational environment determine specific arrangements for airspace control during multinational operations. Effective coordination among multinational forces is essential, and all multinational aircraft involved in the operation should appear on the daily ATO.

Unmanned Aircraft.

Unmanned aircraft (UA) may be operated in the airspace control area by each joint force component, multinational forces, and other government agencies. The established principles of airspace management used in manned flight operations will normally apply to UA, but since UA may be difficult to visually acquire may not always provide a clear radar or electronic signature, UA operations require special considerations in terms of airspace control and usage.

Theater Missiles.

Theater missiles are standoff weapons fired from a launch point on a preprogrammed flight profile to a designated target. Because these missiles have a small radar cross-section, they are difficult to track with normal radar units conducting airspace control, and positive control is not an effective means to these operations from other air operations. It is imperative that procedural ACMs be established in the ATO, ACO, or SPINS.

Airspace Control in Maritime Operations.

In joint maritime operations, specific control and defensive measures may differ from those used in a land-based operation. The joint force maritime component commander (JFMCC) may be designated the control authority for a specific airspace control area or sector. To ensure unity of effort, the commander responsible for maritime airspace control must coordinate with the ACA. In joint operations composed of adjacent maritime and land environments, specific control and defensive measures may be a composite of those measures normally employed in each environment. The JFC for such operations needs to ensure detailed coordination of control and defensive measures among component commanders.

High-Density Airspace Control Zone Integration with Other Airspace Coordinating Measures.

In some cases, the operational environment may require an airspace/fires density level that exceeds the capability of a single high-density airspace control zone (HIDACZ) controlling authority. One method to prevent overloading the controlling authority is to establish another ACM (restricted operations area, HIDACZ, etc.) above or adjacent to the HIDACZ, controlled by another agency or component.

Airspace Control Execution By Phase

Phase 0 — Shape.

The shape phase includes normal and routine military airspace activities to deter potential adversaries and ensure or solidify relationships with friends and allies. Activities are designed to ensure success by shaping perceptions and influencing the behavior of adversaries and allies, developing allied and friendly military capabilities, improving information exchange and intelligence sharing, and providing US forces with peacetime and contingency airspace access. The host nation (HN) retains ACA and joint forces primarily use existing international or HN airspace procedures or guidelines. The JFC may not designate a standing ACA during this phase, but should appoint a lead agent for coordinating the resolution of issues related to airspace management, air traffic control, terminal instrument procedures, and navigation aids. Joint force airspace planners ensure continuation of routine flight operations, establish relationships with key operational area airspace authorities, develop airspace control plans in preparation for future operations, and build planning expertise.

Phase I — Deter.

Transition to phase I begins with a crisis situation requiring joint force action and crisis action planning. Airspace planning is refined, entailing coordination with international and multiple national authorities and is politically sensitive. Release of airspace planning information may entail OPSEC issues but may also have a deterrent or deceptive effect, and should be treated as a strategic consideration. This phase normally is a demonstration of joint force capabilities and is largely characterized by preparatory actions to facilitate execution of subsequent operational phases. The ACA (or lead agent for airspace management) establishes a dedicated airspace planning team to finalize the ACP, coordinates with the AADC for AADP deconfliction, and develops the ACO for current and future operations. The ACP should contain procedures to integrate military and civil ATC resources; HN agreements that could impact air operations must be considered. Proper coordination with civil air operations is especially important.

Phase II — Seize the Initiative.

Transition to phase II may be accomplished on the JFC's initiative or in response to enemy attack. The ACP should contain instructions to transition from peacetime to combat in simple, clear steps. Redesign of airspace or notification of impending changes to airspace control could signal a pending operation so timing for airspace transition should be considered. Joint air operations play a critical role seizing the initiative or gaining access to a theater or JOA. Integrating the airspace control function with DCA and offensive counterair (OCA) operations is especially critical during efforts to gain air superiority. The JFACC is typically the supported commander for the counterair effort in the operational area and integrates OCA and DCA to achieve air superiority, and also normally is the supported commander for the JFC's overall air interdiction effort. The joint force land component commander (JFLCC), if designated or one or more land component commanders will normally become the supported commanders for their AOs during the latter stages of phase II. The ACP and ACO are fully coordinated with supporting components, coalition partners, and HN air and air defense forces. Phase II airspace control planning should fully integrate fires from all friendly and coalition forces. A key role of the ACP is to define the processes to propose, approve, modify, and promulgate ACMs and FSCMs.

Phase III — Dominate.

Phase III includes the full employment of joint force capabilities and continues the appropriate sequencing of forces into the operational area as quickly as possible. When an operation or campaign is focused on conventional enemy forces, the "dominate" phase normally concludes with decisive operations that drive an enemy to culmination and achieve the JFC's operational objectives. The ACP/ATO/ACO and SPINS should be updated to include responsibilities and authorities (including special operations forces and coalition) for designated areas within JFLCC/JFMCC AOs, procedures for forward operating bases (FOBs) and airfields, ATC/air traffic service at FOBs, ATC/air traffic service at captured airfields, area air defense and short-range air defense integration behind the FSCL and FLOT, and fixed wing, UA, and rotary wing deconfliction methods. Airspace control elements should expect a significant increase in the number of indirect fires in the JFLCC/JFMCC AO, and to effectively integrate fires and airspace control, airspace control elements should determine which ACMs must also be protected by an airspace coordination area or air corridor and coordinate accordingly. Airspace planners should minimize the number of combined ACM/FSCM requests so as not to overly restrict fires, and fires planners should understand there are some areas in which the JFC cannot accept the risk of mixing fires and manned aircraft. Missions such as air assaults, airborne assaults, and other incursions into enemy territory require specific airspace control coordination.

Phase IV — Stabilize.

Phase IV operations ensure that the threat (military or political) is reduced to a manageable level that can be controlled by the HN authority and that the situation which led to the original crisis does not recur. The joint force may be required to perform local governance until legitimate local entities are functioning, and ACA may be required to perform roles associated with HN aviation authorities. A key requirement is to plan for an effective transfer of airspace control from the joint force to the HN in phase V. The ACP should address airspace access criteria for non-JFC organizations, joint force to civil airspace priority, and identification and acceptance of associated civil airspace operating risks. Reducing threats to air operations and establishing security are required. Normally, a government or civil organization will handle the planning for reconstituting the HN ACS, but the ACA may be the only one able to assume this role in some cases. The pre-conflict HN airspace control structure should provide the basic airspace end-state concept unless destroyed or deemed ineffective. From an ACA's perspective, the end of phase IV and the beginning of phase V milestone is reached when the framework of the HN ACS is in place and the HN is ready to assume ACA.

Phase V — Enable Civil Authority.

This phase is characterized by joint force support to legitimate civil governance. Depending upon the level of HN capacity, joint force activities may be at the behest of that authority or they may be under its direction. The joint force will perform key airspace functions either as the delegated ACA or as supporting airspace service provider under the HN aviation authority. Phase V could result as a normal phased transition from phase IV or as joint force support to a humanitarian relief effort, natural disaster, etc. During this phase HN aviation regulations and guidance are the authoritative source for airspace control procedures. Airspace control personnel may be required to provide Service-specific controllers, ACS, liaisons, or trainers to support HN authorities. Setting the conditions and milestones for the relief of joint forces and the reestablishment of effective HN airspace control is crucial. Risk is a fundamental consideration of airspace control, and the JFC's acceptable level of risk for all airspace users (including fires) should be clearly delineated in the ACP.

CONCLUSION

This publication provides doctrine for the planning, execution, and assessment of airspace control during joint operations across the full range of military operations. It also discusses airspace control across the phases of military operations, emphasizing transitions from, and back to, civilian controlled airspace.

CHAPTER I
INTRODUCTION

"Gulf lesson one is the value of air power…we must retain combat superiority in the skies."

**President George H. W. Bush
29 May 1991**

1. General

a. This joint publication (JP) prescribes doctrine for joint airspace control in the operational area. The prescribed doctrine is broadly stated to fit a wide range of situations **requiring military control of airspace.** International agreements, enemy, and friendly force structures and deployments, commander's concept of operations (CONOPS), and operational environments in foreign countries, on the high seas, and within amphibious objective areas (AOAs) may necessitate different specific arrangements for joint airspace control.

b. In today's complex airspace environment, civilian use of airspace will likely occur alongside ongoing military operations. Civilian airliners, nongovernmental organizations (NGOs), and relief agencies will require use of airspace to continue their associated operations. The advent of military integrated air defense systems, cruise missiles, and unmanned aircraft systems (UASs) further complicates airspace control requirements. Indirect fire systems are also airspace users and today range higher and farther than ever before. These increased user demands require an integrated airspace control system (ACS) that facilitates mission accomplishment while reducing the possibility of fratricide.

c. **This publication outlines fundamental principles, relationships, and broad operational-level guidelines.** It is not intended to limit commanders' authority over and responsibility for their forces, but is intended to provide the basic framework upon which to build an ACS for an operational area.

d. The joint force commander (JFC) will normally designate a joint force air component commander (JFACC) as the commander for joint air operations. In addition to a JFACC, the JFC also normally designates an area air defense commander (AADC) and an airspace control authority (ACA). When the JFC designates a JFACC, the JFC also normally designates the JFACC as the AADC and ACA, because the three functions are so integral to one another. The ACA is responsible for planning, coordinating, and developing airspace control procedures and operating the ACS. When the situation dictates, the JFC may designate a separate ACA and/or AADC. **In those circumstances where separate commanders are required and designated, close coordination is essential for unity of effort, prevention of fratricide, and deconfliction of joint air operations.**

e. Upon indication of, or receipt of, tasking from higher commanders, the ACA develops a specific airspace control plan (ACP) that is approved by the JFC. The plan should take into consideration the likelihood of multinational operations, as well as the need for developing policies and procedures that foster compatibility and interoperability of support systems and methods to accommodate potential civilian air operations. US forces participating in multinational operations may be subject to command arrangements and authorities established in international agreements. The ACP should be closely integrated with the JFC-approved area air defense plan (AADP) developed by the AADC.

2. Joint Airspace Control

a. Airspace control increases combat effectiveness **by promoting the safe, efficient, and flexible use of airspace with minimum restraint placed upon the airspace users.** Joint airspace control includes coordinating, integrating, and regulating airspace to increase operational effectiveness. Effective airspace control reduces the risk of fratricide, enhances air defense operations, and permits greater flexibility of joint operations. Airspace control operations may begin prior to (and continue after) combat operations and may transition through varying degrees of civil and military authority. **The JFC defines the relationship between the ACA and component commanders.** The ACA has authority to approve, amend, or disapprove airspace requests for the designated operational area in accordance with JFC guidance and objectives. The ACA does not have the authority to approve, disapprove, or deny combat operations. That authority is only vested in operational commanders. If the ACA and an affected component commander are unable to obtain agreement on an airspace issue, the issue will be referred to the JFC for resolution.

b. **Airspace control is essential to military operational effectiveness in accomplishing JFC objectives across the range of military operations.** Given the speed and physical characteristics of flight, airspace coordinating measures (ACMs) are integrated into operations to deconflict airspace users and decrease the potential for fratricide. Available technical capabilities such as surveillance, navigation, and communications between airspace users and airspace control agencies often determine the required ACMs. In general, lower technical capabilities result in decreased airspace efficiency potential. Conversely, higher technical capabilities result in increased airspace efficiency potential. Airspace control is extremely dynamic and situational, and it needs to be flexible and responsive enough to accommodate users with varied technical capabilities in order to optimize airspace use. **Airspace control provides the JFC operational flexibility to employ forces effectively.** Fundamental considerations are shown in Figure I-1.

3. Basic Principles

Airspace is a crucial part of the operational environment and is used by all components of the joint and multinational forces. A high concentration of friendly surface, subsurface, and air-launched weapon systems must share this airspace without unnecessarily hindering the application of combat power in accordance with the JFC's intent. **The primary goal of airspace control is to enhance effectiveness of the joint force and increase the safety of joint air operations.** Basic principles of airspace control are listed in Figure I-2 and described below.

FUNDAMENTAL CONSIDERATIONS OF AIRSPACE CONTROL

- The need for each component within the joint force to operate a variety of aircraft and weapon systems, both high and low speed, rotary- and fixed-wing (manned and unmanned).

- The need for each component to use the airspace with maximum freedom consistent with the degree of risk operationally acceptable to the joint force commander.

- The need for airspace control activities to be performed in congruence with air defense operations to integrate and synchronize surface-to-air defense weapons and air defense aircraft for maximum effectiveness.

- The need to discriminate quickly and effectively between friendly, neutral, and enemy air operations, vehicles, and personnel.

- The need for the airspace control system to be responsive to the requirements of the joint force. The airspace control system needs to be capable of supporting high-density traffic and surge operations as may be required by the joint force commander.

- The need for close coordination and integration of surface force operations, supporting fires, air operations, air defense operations, special operations, and airspace control activities.

- The need to accommodate US, host-nation, and multinational airspace control activities.

- The need to recognize the saturation levels and limitations of airspace control networks.

- The need for temporary restrictive airspace coordinating measures for certain areas of airspace to allow subordinate commanders maximum freedom of action.

- The need to incorporate, in detail, coordinated offensive operations using electronic warfare elements, strike aircraft, and missiles to ensure that defensive elements of procedures of the force do not unacceptably inhibit or degrade offensive capabilities.

- The need to ensure that the airspace control network remains survivable and effective.

- The need to provide maximum opportunities to employ deception measures.

- The need to standardize communications data, format, and language requirements in multinational operations to reduce the possibility of differences in interpretation, translation, or application of airspace control procedures during multinational operations.

- The need to support 24-hour operations in all weather and environmental conditions.

Figure I-1. Fundamental Considerations of Airspace Control

BASIC PRINCIPLES OF AIRSPACE CONTROL

- Unity of effort requires the airspace control system and associated procedures to be fully coordinated, integrated, and centrally planned by the airspace control authority.
- Reduce the risk of fratricide and optimize the effectiveness of air defense.
- Centralized airspace planning facilitates meeting joint force commander priorities.
- Decentralized execution gives subordinate commanders the flexibility to execute their missions effectively.
- Maintain close liaison and coordination among all airspace users.
- Require common airspace control procedures, which include procedural and/or positive control measures.
- Require reliable, jam-resistant, beyond line of sight, and secure communications networks.
- Require survivable, integrated, and redundant airspace control systems.
- Respond to developing threat conditions and to the unfolding operation.
- Airspace control functions rely on airspace management resources, but they are different than the air traffic control environment.
- Emphasize flexibility and simplicity.
- Airspace control systems must be integrated to the maximum extent practical.
- Support 24-hour operations in all weather and environmental conditions.
- Require appropriate training for effective and safe airspace control operations.

Figure I-2. Basic Principles of Airspace Control

a. The ACS must support JFC objectives and facilitate **unity of effort.** A coordinated and integrated ACS is essential to the conduct of successful operations. In many operations, wide-ranging interagency and NGO involvement may challenge unity of command; nevertheless, unity of effort should be preserved to ensure common focus and mutually supporting actions. Airspace is a finite commodity which requires effective management and prioritization for use.

b. A major reason for close coordination between airspace control, air traffic control (ATC), and air defense elements is to **reduce the risk of fratricide and increase the effectiveness of air defense.** Identification requirements for airspace control must be compatible with those for air defense. Airspace control, air defense, ATC, supporting procedures, equipment, and terminology need to be compatible, mutually supporting, integrated, and interoperable.

c. The designated ACA maintains situational awareness of the airspace environment, while focusing on the designated operational area and JFC mission requirements, and is best suited to balance competing airspace needs against the conflict. **Centralized airspace planning** by the ACA facilitates meeting JFC priorities with a fully coordinated and integrated ACS. **Decentralized execution** allows subordinate commanders to take the initiative and increase airspace control effectiveness through real-time airspace integration during execution. The ACS and procedures must be flexible enough to permit decentralized execution to the extent warranted by the operational environment. In those situations where there is one theater-wide ACA supporting more than one subordinate JFC (more than one joint operations area, [JOA]), a separate and distinct ACP and airspace control order (ACO) will need to be developed and then approved by the respective subordinate JFC.

d. **Close liaison and coordination among all airspace users inside and outside the JOA** is necessary to promote timely and accurate information flow to airspace managers. Effective liaison and coordination directly relate to the success of the campaign or operation.

e. **Airspace control procedures provide flexibility through an effective combination of positive and procedural control measures.** The control structure encourages close coordination between joint force components to allow rapid concentration of combat power. As operations progress through different phases, the ACS adapts to changing requirements and priorities.

(1) **Procedural control relies on common procedures,** designated airspace, and promulgated instructions by an authorized control agency to deconflict and activate ATC areas, ACMs, fire support coordination measures (FSCMs), and air defense control measures. Procedural control activates the airspace by defined volume and time through standard ACMs or updates to weapons control status. This serves to deconflict the defined airspace and aircraft from other airspace users. When appropriate communications exist, an authorized airspace control agency can provide procedural control instructions in real time to increase operational flexibility for airspace users. Procedural control establishes the minimum common criteria and concepts for airspace control. Although potentially not as efficient as positive control, procedural control provides effective airspace system capabilities for low density airspace situations and in areas that lack positive control coverage. **Procedural control measures need to be uncomplicated** and readily accessible to all forces and disseminated in the ACP, ACO, and special instructions (SPINS) of the air tasking order (ATO). Use of these documents is essential for the planning and integration of manned and unmanned aircraft (UA) operations.

(2) **Positive control relies on surveillance, accurate identification, and effective communications between a designated airspace control agency and all airspace users.** It is normally conducted by agencies equipped with radar; identification, friend or foe (IFF) interrogators and receivers; beacons; track processing computers; digital data links; and communications equipment. The minimum requirements for surveillance, identification, and communications equipment will vary in each theater, but are likely to be driven by a combination of military and civil aviation regulations and the

level of risk the JFC is willing to accept. **Positive control requires two primary conditions: the means to locate and identify airspace users and the ability to maintain continuous communications with them for required control instructions.** Positive control procedures must include provisions for transition to procedural control if positive control systems are degraded or become unavailable. They must also take into account differences between civil and military communications and surveillance systems.

(3) **There is a continuum of efficiency, level of effort, resources required, and risk between procedural and positive control.** Uncontrolled airspace exerts a small drain on resources, but increases risk. Standing ACMs, such as a restricted operations zone (ROZ), incrementally increase control and resources required, but do not provide the best mitigation for risk. Full military or civilian positive control provides the best mitigation for risk, but has a large cost in resources. This comparison assumes a constant volume of air traffic. Ideally, the entire airspace control area would be under positive control with radar and communication coverage. However, limited resources or other factors, such as terrain and lack of integrated technology, may make this goal unrealistic. Airspace planners should determine where the JFC's tolerance for risk is lowest, or the needs for efficiency are highest, and establish the appropriate combination of positive and/or procedural control in those areas first. In areas where positive control isn't feasible, standing ACMs should establish the minimum standard for airspace control. These standing measures form a crucial backup in the event positive control capability is diminished. Figure I-3 depicts these relationships.

f. The ACS should have a **reliable, integrated, jam-resistant, and secure communications network.** However, care should be exercised to avoid control procedures that rely heavily on voice communications. Emphasis should be placed on simple, flexible airspace management procedures. Airspace management provisions should allow for possible degradation in control capability. In this manner, flexibility and responsiveness are preserved. Coordinated and detailed planning is required to ensure that communications systems and procedures are compatible among all airspace managers and users.

g. **Air control assets comprising the overall ACS need to be survivable and redundant** because they are likely to be prime targets for an attacker.

h. The structure of the ACS needs to be **responsive to developing threats and to the unfolding operation.** The design, responsiveness, and procedures of the ACS should support the rapid massing of combat power.

i. Airspace control functions rely on **airspace management resources,** but these functions are separate and distinct from ATC. However, ATC equipment, procedures, and personnel are integral to any ACS and must be able to communicate and coordinate within such a system.

j. The system developed for airspace control is generally based on compromise between a wide variety of conflicting demands for airspace use. **Flexibility and**

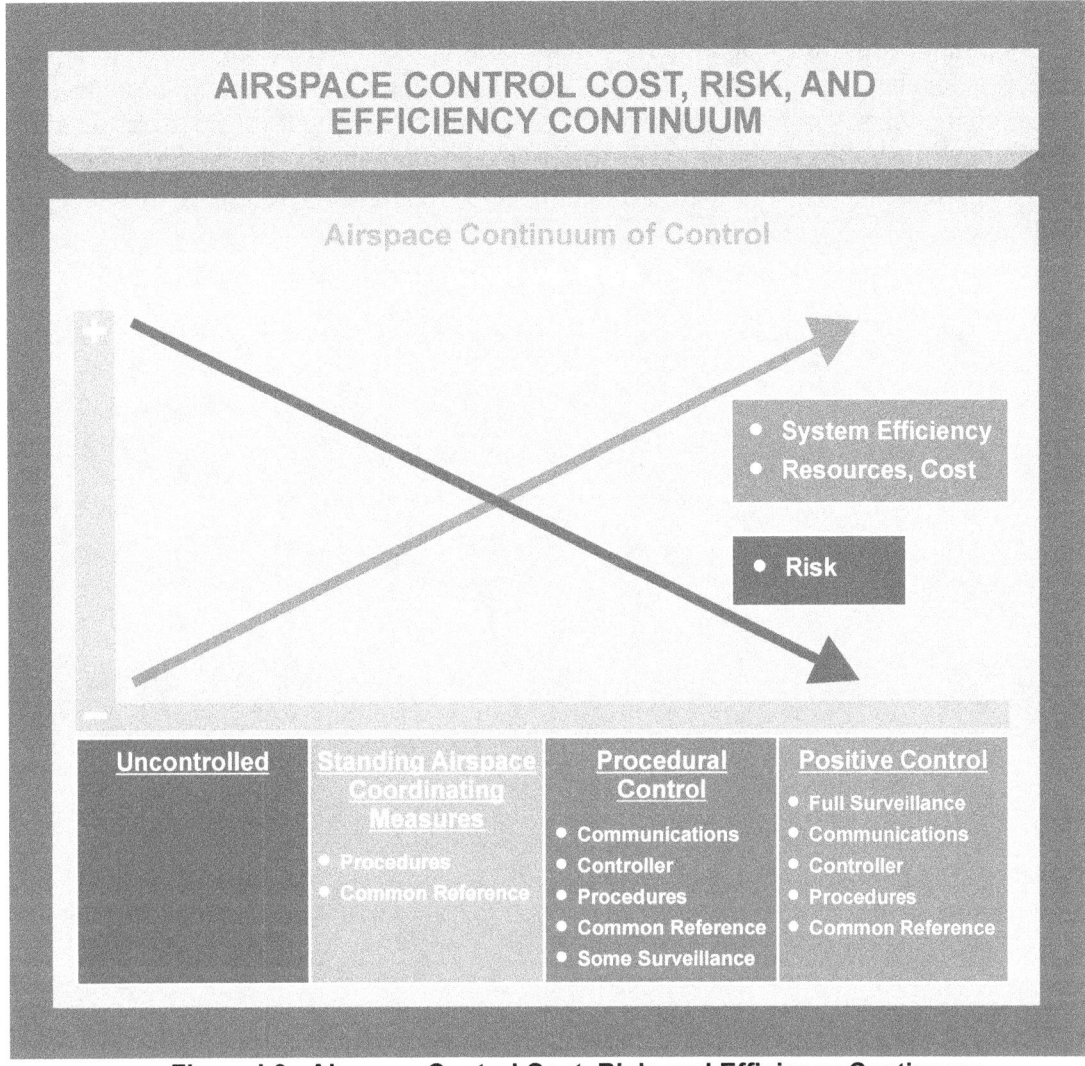

Figure I-3. Airspace Control Cost, Risk, and Efficiency Continuum

simplicity must be emphasized throughout to maximize the effectiveness of forces operating within the system. This flexibility must include the ability to incorporate a civil air traffic structure where no host nation (HN) capability exists.

k. ACSs should be **interoperable and integrated.** Integrated ACSs are synergistic and more effective than the sum of their parts.

l. Airspace control needs to **support 24-hour operations in all weather and environmental conditions.**

m. **Effective and safe operations in today's complex airspace require appropriate training for joint airspace users and joint ACS personnel.** Core airspace training is primarily a Service component responsibility with theater-specific training as required. To provide a realistic training environment, ACS components (such as the theater air control system and ATC) should be exercised as an overall system rather than as separate entities. Exercises and simulations involving multiple agencies and users across the range of military operations provide complexity and realism to effectively train airspace agencies and users. Joint, coalition, other government agencies, and international civil airspace elements should be incorporated whenever possible to validate emerging interoperability capabilities. Airspace control units should establish procedural agreements and establish required communication links to ensure effective interagency coordination.

CHAPTER II
ORGANIZATION AND COORDINATION

"Generally, management of the many is the same as management of the few. It is a matter of organization."

Sun Tzu

1. General

a. Consistent with the provisions of JP 1, *Doctrine for the Armed Forces of the United States*, **a JFC has the authority to organize forces to accomplish the assigned mission based on the CONOPS.** The organization of forces will depend on the mission assigned, the manner in which the mission is to be fulfilled, and the capabilities and strength of the component elements of the forces assigned. Consequently, the organizational form of the ACS may vary.

b. **The following organizational arrangements may apply to airspace control for joint forces.** When circumstances dictate, appropriate modification may be prescribed by the JFC.

2. Organization

The following descriptions of broad duties are central to effective airspace control. Understanding the roles of the JFC, the JFACC, other component commanders, the ACA, and the AADC is essential. Other key airspace control definitions are addressed in Annex B to Appendix B, "Airspace Coordinating and Fire Support Coordination Measures," and in the glossary.

a. **Joint Force Commander. The JFC is responsible for airspace control in the JOA.** The ACP and ACO express how the airspace will be used to support mission accomplishment.

b. **Joint Force Air Component Commander.** The JFC will normally designate a JFACC and assign responsibilities. The JFACC's responsibilities normally include, but are not limited to: planning, coordinating, and monitoring joint air operations, and the allocation and tasking of joint air operations forces based on the JFC's CONOPS and air apportionment decision. **The JFC normally designates the JFACC as the AADC and ACA since air defense and airspace control are so integral to joint air operations.** The JFACC may be designated the ACA by the JFC, or the JFC may designate a separate ACA. In either case, the ACA is responsible for planning, coordinating, and developing airspace control procedures and operating the ACS. The air operations directive (AOD) provides the JFACC's guidance for each ATO and the successive planning steps. Furthermore, this document conveys the JFC's guidance with respect to acceptable levels of risk, usually based on mission type orders. This gives the operational level planners the information they need to allocate sorties to meet JFC objectives within imposed risk constraints. When the situation dictates, the JFC may designate a separate AADC and/or ACA. In those joint operations where separate commanders are required and designated, close coordination is essential for unity of effort, prevention of fratricide, and deconfliction of joint air operations.

For additional details on the organization and functioning of a JFACC, see JP 3-30, Command and Control for Joint Air Operations.

c. **Component Commanders. Component commanders advise the JFC on the employment of component forces** and the direction and control of those forces. Each component commander plans and executes a portion of the total air effort and interacts with other components. **Subject to the authority of the JFC, each component commander within a joint force:**

(1) **Employs air defense weapons systems** in accordance with the rules of engagement (ROE), the AADP, and other operational guidance.

(2) **Coordinates, deconflicts, and integrates operations with other component commanders when appropriate.** Coordination for airspace control may be facilitated through collocation of key airspace control, air defense, and fire support coordination agencies. When collocation is not possible, such facilities need to be connected with appropriate secure communications, and liaison personnel should be exchanged. This coordination is especially important during the planning phases of an operation.

(3) **Forwards requests for ACMs and FSCMs** in accordance with the ACP.

(4) **Develops detailed airspace control instructions, plans, and procedures** in accordance with ACP guidance. These detailed instructions, plans, and procedures must be consistent with JFC-approved airspace control guidance in the ACP.

(5) **Provides necessary facilities and personnel** for airspace control functions in assigned areas and identifies these facilities and personnel for inclusion in the ACP.

d. **Airspace Control Authority.** The ACA develops airspace control policies and procedures for all airspace users. The ACA establishes an ACS based upon JFC requirements and integrates the ACS with the HN. The ACA coordinates and integrates airspace use under JFC authority. **The ACP is a directive for all joint force elements using the airspace to include manned and unmanned aircraft and indirect fires.** Implementation of the ACP begins with the distribution of the ACO, and is executed when components and users comply with the ACO as described in JP 3-30, *Command and Control for Joint Air Operations.* The ACP establishes the ACS, the control nodes, and airspace procedures. The ACO implements the ACP. ACA responsibilities are summarized in Figure II-1.

AIRSPACE CONTROL AUTHORITY RESPONSIBILITIES

- Coordinate and integrate the airspace.
- Develop policies and procedures for coordinated airspace control required among units within the operational area.
- Establish an airspace control system that is responsive to the needs of the joint force commander, provide for integration of the airspace control system with that of the host nation, assist in establishing a civil structure where none exists, and coordinate and deconflict user requirements.
- Develop the airspace control plan and, after joint force commander approval, distribute it throughout the operational area. Implement the airspace control plan through the airspace control order.
- Provide necessary facilities and personnel for airspace control functions in assigned areas and identify these facilities and personnel for inclusion in the airspace control plan.

Figure II-1. Airspace Control Authority Responsibilities

e. **Area Air Defense Commander. The AADC is responsible for defensive counterair (DCA) operations, which include both air and missile threats.** The AADC identifies ACMs that support and enhance DCA operations, identifies required airspace management systems, establishes procedures for systems to operate within the airspace, and incorporates them into the ACS.

3. **Liaison Requirements**

Liaison requirements will vary based upon the nature of the mission, size of the force, and various operation and mission variables; therefore, the proper identification of liaison requirements is a key planning and command and control (C2) consideration.

4. **Airspace Control Plan**

The ACP establishes procedures for the ACS in the operational area. An example of the topics that should be considered when developing an ACP is provided in Appendix A, "Airspace Control Plan Development Considerations." **The JFC approves the ACP.** To provide effective operational procedures **the ACP and AADP must be integrated with the JFC's operation plan (OPLAN) and orders.** The ACP considers procedures and interfaces with the international or regional air traffic systems necessary to effectively support air operations, augmenting forces and JFC objectives. Consequently, the ACP should be preplanned, to the degree possible, and be put in a simplified, understandable format. Because the airspace control area normally coincides with air defense boundaries, coordination between airspace control and area air defense operations is essential. Key factors to consider are listed in Figure II-2.

AIRSPACE CONTROL PLAN CONSIDERATIONS

- Procedures that include rules of engagement and disposition of air defense weapon systems, such as air defense fighters, air defense artillery, surface-to-air missiles, and air defense command and control operations.

- Limitations or adverse conditions within air, land, and maritime situations in the operational area, such as existing equipment limitations, electronic warfare, and communications system requirements that may adversely affect the airspace control plan.

- Anticipated restricted areas based on initial deployment of friendly air, land, maritime, and special operations forces and bases.

- Existing air traffic control areas, base defense zones, controlled or uncontrolled airspace, and overflight of neutral nations.

- Mission profiles; combat radii; and identification, friend or foe (IFF), or other identification capability of aircraft that will operate in the operational area.

- Enemy air defense weapons capabilities and deployment.

- Electronic attack and deception capabilities.

- Emergency procedures for aircraft experiencing difficulties (including IFF problems).

- Procedures for day or night operations and for aircraft experiencing adverse weather.

- En route and terminal-area air traffic control procedures for aircraft transiting to and from the operational area.

- Procedures to support surge operations requiring high volumes of air traffic.

- Enemy offensive air capabilities. Additionally, the vulnerability of friendly aircraft to enemy surface-to-air missiles and the vulnerability of friendly surface-based air defenses to enemy long-range indirect fires are important planning and execution considerations.

- Procedures, routes, and restricted areas for air mobility assets performing direct combat support of forces, logistic resupply, aerial refueling, or aeromedical evacuation.

- Civil air traffic corridors and procedures.

- Provisions for fire support coordination measures.

Figure II-2. Airspace Control Plan Considerations

a. The ACP should be **coordinated with HN** representatives if appropriate and available.

b. Planning factors to be addressed when developing the ACP include familiarity with the basic OPLAN or operation order (OPORD), combined with knowledge of HN and multinational considerations, understanding the operational and mission variables, familiarity with the capabilities and procedures of civil and military airspace management systems, and general locations of friendly and enemy forces.

c. **The ACP needs to support an orderly transition between peacetime and combat operations.** Such a transition could occur during a period of increasing and/or decreasing tensions or suddenly without much warning.

d. **The ACP specifies ACMs and FSCMs to be used in the operational area** and how these measures will be distributed and implemented. The ACP should provide guidance on what FSCMs will be placed in the ACO. The ACP should also provide guidance on component-unique ACMs, terms, or graphics that may be included in the ACO.

e. The ACP provides procedures to fully integrate the resources of military ATC facilities responsible for terminal-area airspace control or en route ATC. **ATC facilities are interfaced and linked with ACS communications to form a system that fosters the safe and efficient flow of air traffic.**

f. **The AADP includes detailed engagement procedures.** Airspace control and area air defense operations should have plans for operations in a degraded communications environment. Detailed engagement procedures and decentralized weapons control procedures (as applied to air defense) are key to operations in a degraded environment. **Integration of air defense forces within the overall ACP is critical to effective airspace control.** The geographic arrangement of weapons and the location of specific types of air defense operations, as well as specific procedures for identification of aircraft, are critical factors to include in the ACP.

g. The ACP and AADP are distributed to all forces providing intertheater or intratheater air support. Not understanding or following the ACP and AADP may result in hazardous air traffic situations, cause confusion between aircraft and control agencies, and increase the risk of fratricide.

5. Airspace Control Order

The ACP provides general guidance for the control of the airspace, but the ACO implements specific control procedures for established time periods. The ACO is an order that provides the details of the approved requests for ACMs and FSCMs. It is published either as part of the ATO or as a separate document. **The ACO defines and establishes airspace for military operations as coordinated by the ACA.** It notifies all agencies of the effective time of activation and the composite structure of the airspace to be used. The ACO may include ACMs and FSCMs such as air routes, base defense zones (BDZs), coordinating measures/lines, drop zones, pickup points, restricted areas, carrier control zones, and other areas. A change to the ACO should be distributed whenever a new area is established or an existing area deleted. Timely promulgation of ACO changes to all airspace users, to include multinational forces, is essential to avoid fratricide and increase operational effectiveness.

6. Airspace Control Order Development

a. While the ACP provides general guidance on the airspace control function, the ACO implements airspace control procedures for specified time periods and may be distributed as part of the ATO or as a separate document. Normally, the ACO is published and distributed daily and contains ACMs, procedural control instructions, and the airspace required to support the corresponding ATO. The ACO activates and deactivates procedural control measures and updates positive control measures.

b. Procedures for developing and updating the ACO are included in the ACP. Normally, component commanders consolidate, deconflict, and forward their airspace requests to the ACA by a specified time for further consolidation with other inputs. All inputs are integrated and conflicts among the components are resolved. Planners should be aware that not all information that goes into the ACO is the result of a request for airspace. Guidance should be given, depending on the level and the number of forces in the operational area, on what other information should be included, e.g., FSCMs and other control measures.

c. The JFC may elect to delegate specific authority for airspace control to the component commanders through ACP guidelines. The JFC may also elect to task the component commanders to generate individual ACOs for their assigned sectors. Regardless, the ACA is tasked with providing continuity along sector boundaries and ensuring integration of each sector authority's ACO within the ACP guidelines.

d. The ACA remains responsible for airspace control for the entire operational area. The decision to develop a single ACO or multiple ACOs will be situation-dependent. Normally, a single ACO is used.

7. The Joint Air Tasking Cycle

a. The joint air tasking process provides for the effective and efficient employment of joint air capabilities and forces. This process provides an iterative, cyclic process for the planning, apportionment, allocation, coordination, tasking, and execution of joint air missions and sorties within the guidance of the JFC. The process accommodates changing tactical situations or JFC guidance as well as requests for support from other component commanders. **The joint air tasking process is a systematic cycle that focuses joint air efforts on supporting operational requirements.** Much of the day-to-day tasking cycle is conducted through an interrelated series of information exchanges and active involvement in plan development, target development, air execution, and assessment, which provide a means of requesting and scheduling joint air missions.

b. **Planners must develop airspace control and air defense instructions in sufficient detail to allow components to plan and execute all air missions listed in the ATO.** These directions enable combat operations without undue restrictions, balancing combat effectiveness with the safe, orderly, and expeditious use of airspace. Instructions provide for quick coordination of task assignment and reassignment and direct aircraft identification and engagement procedures and ROE appropriate to the nature of the threat. These instructions should also consider the volume of friendly air traffic, friendly air defense requirements, IFF technology, weather, and adversary capabilities. Instructions are contained in the SPINS and in the ACO, and are updated as frequently as required. **The ATO, ACO, and SPINS provide operational and tactical direction at appropriate levels of detail.**

c. **The ATO is the OPORD or mission assignment for all aircraft missions flown** under the control of the JFACC **in the operational area and shows all missions operating in the operational area during the effective time period.** Other air missions not under the control of the JFACC may be added to the ATO to provide visibility for overall coordination and deconfliction. A timely ATO is critical — joint force components conduct their planning and operations based on a timely, executable ATO and are dependent on its information.

d. In some theaters, numerous airspace procedures and airspace usages are published in the SPINS. The SPINS include a section on airspace procedures. Other SPINS sections will include tanker procedures, cruise missile procedures, etc., as required. The SPINS may include ROE and combat identification criteria for air defense along with any additional guidance/directives/information for weapons system operators and/or aircrews such as HN restrictions, BDZ procedures, and special weapons systems control procedures. SPINS are published as baseline SPINS, weekly SPINS, and daily SPINS.

For further discussion of the joint air tasking cycle see JP 3-30, Command and Control for Joint Air Operations.

8. **Communications and Security Considerations**

a. **ACSs should be joint, interoperable, survivable, sustainable, and redundant.** The ACS should be jam-resistant with secure C2 networks. The ACS should allow users to maintain situational awareness and effectively respond to evolving enemy situation and friendly air operations. Timely integration of sensor data; intelligence, surveillance, and reconnaissance (ISR) information; aircraft, ground, maritime, and special operations forces (SOF); and networked inputs between authorized airspace control agencies and C2 nodes to develop a common operational picture (COP) provides crucial situational awareness for airspace agencies, users, and decisionmakers.

b. The purpose of security is to never permit the enemy to acquire an unexpected advantage. Secure ACSs including sensors, communications, data processing, and common operating databases are crucial to effective airspace control capabilities. Information assurance (IA) programs such as communications security, physical security, emissions security, and network defense are methods to protect ACSs and information. **Due to the US military's dependency on and the general vulnerability of electronic information and its supporting systems, IA is essential to airspace control.** Considerations for operations security (OPSEC) must be applied when developing communication policies and procedures.

c. ACSs, especially voice radio communications, are susceptible to frequency jammers, data emitters, or other radio transmitters operating in the same segment of the electromagnetic spectrum. Such interference can result in degraded communications between airspace control agencies and users creating potential safety of flight and/or fratricide situations. Potential sources of interference should be identified and alternate frequencies allocated and alternate means of communication established. Additionally, specific communications outage procedures should be clearly defined in the event communications are lost or jammed entirely. Airspace management planning and execution must be integrated with spectrum management throughout all phases of operations.

CHAPTER III
AIRSPACE CONTROL PLANNING CONSIDERATIONS

"The first and absolute requirement of strategic air power in this war was control of the air in order to carry out sustained operations without prohibitive losses."

General Carl A. "Tooey" Spaatz
Air Force Chief of Staff, 1947

1. Airspace Considerations by Phase

a. **Phasing provides an orderly schedule of military operations and indicates preplanned shifts in priorities and intent.** Phasing is a way to view and conduct a complex joint operation in manageable parts. The main purpose of phasing is to integrate and synchronize related activities, thereby enhancing flexibility and unity of effort during execution. Phasing may be used to modify the prioritization of airspace control missions and priorities for operations. Phasing is a useful tool to communicate the CONOPS and the shifting priorities between ongoing airspace operations. Airspace planners should consider that all operations will not smoothly transition between phases, and depending on the nature of the conflict, national political objectives, and JFC intent, operations may cease prior to the beginning of phase IV (Stabilize) or phase V (Enable Civil Authority). **It is of the utmost importance to remember that the phasing construct is just a model to start planning efforts. Each and every conflict is different and will not resemble the model at different points in time.**

For more details on phasing see JP 3-0, Joint Operations.

b. Transferring airspace control authority from civilian to military control, adapting the ACS to JFC needs during each phase, and eventually returning it to civil authority are complex tasks requiring joint military, diplomatic, and interagency efforts. Since a crisis may occur unexpectedly, airspace control and management activities should be a part of contingency and crisis action planning from the beginning. For instance, moving C2 and airspace control equipment is a time-phased force and deployment data consideration. Since much of this equipment may deploy (or redeploy) late in the operation due to intertheater airlift (or other lift) limitations, a dynamic plan from the beginning is required to ensure critical airspace control capability.

c. During joint operations, the likely mix of military and commercial air traffic activity during various phases may make airspace control more complex than during combat. In addition, the ACA may transfer airspace control to the HN during these phases which gives the JFC and ACA a less direct voice in the conduct of airspace control for continuing JFC operations. The tasks and responsibilities of ACA may play a role in the support of strategic and operational partnerships as part of theater security cooperation. Figure III-1 depicts notional airspace control authority and the differing priorities and intent between civil and military airspace procedures.

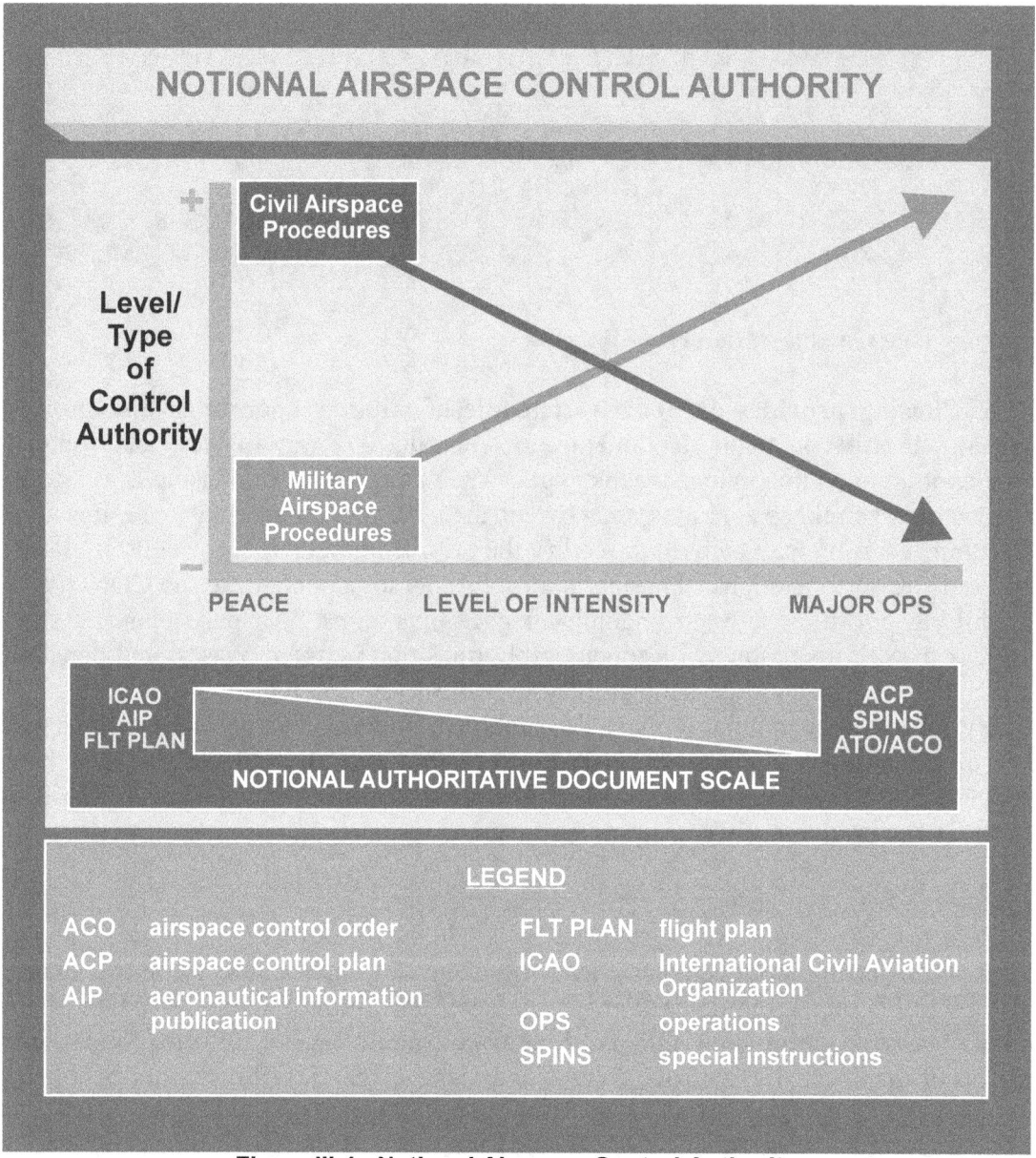

Figure III-1. Notional Airspace Control Authority

d. Noncombat activities across the range of military operations, such as disaster relief or other support to government activities share many of the same characteristics of phase IV or V activities. For instance, a disaster may destroy a nation's airspace control capability and the US Government (USG) may elect to provide assistance until the capability can be restored. The International Civil Aviation Organization (ICAO) has guidelines for airspace practices in the event of a disaster or significant noncombat events and these should be referenced together with existing HN procedures. Coordination with the HN; determination of authorities; interfacing with joint, interagency, and multinational organizations; providing service; and deconflicting military and civilian traffic are all applicable to operations other than combat.

e. Operation NOBLE EAGLE, the homeland air defense operations launched by North American Aerospace Defense Command after the attacks of 11 September 2001, and military support operations after Hurricane Katrina demonstrated the need for a clear understanding of responsibilities and effective coordination between civil and military airspace control agencies during homeland defense or civil support operations. Specific information for homeland airspace coordination considerations is included in JP 3-28, *Civil Support*.

2.   **Airspace Control Risk Considerations**

Risk is a fundamental consideration of airspace control.   Joint doctrine recognizes the need for each Service and functional component to use the airspace with maximum availability consistent with the JFC acceptable level of risk. **The JFC's acceptable level of risk for all airspace users (including fires) should be clearly delineated in the ACP.** During all phases the assumption of risk is a command decision. Definitions of high, moderate, and low risk vary from theater to theater based on the geographic combatant commander's guidance.   In general terms, high risk prioritizes mission accomplishment over the preservation of resources; moderate risk seeks to balance mission accomplishment with potential resource losses and may require slight mission adjustments to achieve objectives; and low risk prioritizes the preservation of resources and may require substantial mission adjustments to achieve objectives. As the volume of airspace users increases, control should be enhanced to keep the level of risk acceptable to the JFC. The ACP should specify areas where high volumes of airspace users are projected and plan for increased control capability.   If an enhanced control capability is not an option, then commanders should understand they are accepting a higher risk of midair collisions and fratricide with indirect fires, manned systems, and UA. Commanders may accept different levels of risk based on the systems involved.   For example, a commander may direct that a higher level of risk be accepted for possible fratricide between indirect fires and some or all UA than between indirect fires and manned aircraft.

3.   **Planning for Joint Airspace Control**

Each operational area has specific operational requirements for airspace control. These requirements must be determined as early as possible and incorporated in the overall joint force planning effort. Political constraints, national and military airspace management systems, and procedures and their capabilities and limitations are important considerations.   ROE, disposition of air defense weapons, fire support plans, and procedures for identification of US and multinational aircraft are also important items to consider. **Every joint/multinational force is different, and the forces assigned will have specific operational requirements for airspace.** The following broad principles of planning (see Figure III-2) are essential to effective airspace control:

Figure III-2. Principles for Planning Airspace Control for Military Operations

a. **Interoperability.** Airspace control should be exercised in the joint and multinational environments during peacetime and in conflict. Planning for airspace control includes considerations for interoperability of equipment, as well as personnel and terminology.

b. **Mass and Timing.** Planning considerations should include the aircraft traffic volume anticipated for the operations, the timing constraints placed on those operations, as well as requirements.

c. **Unity of Effort.** Liaison requirements, especially between joint force components and multinational forces, should be identified and exercised prior to hostilities. Representatives from different components and multinational forces need to integrate information flow throughout the system and provide expertise to the designated ACA.

d. **Integrated Planning Cycles.** The airspace planning cycle should be integrated with the overall planning cycle for the joint operation or campaign. Once input from all organizations involved in the operation is consolidated, the final ACP is devised and disseminated to users of the ACO. The ACP can be added as an appendix to the operations annex to the joint force OPLAN or OPORD.

e. **Degraded Operations.** Plans should anticipate the effects of electronic warfare (EW), combat losses, and communications degradation on system operations. An effective ACS needs to plan for the full spectrum of communications from no degradation to full degradation and should consider degradation due to changing environmental conditions.

4. **Integration of Joint Airspace Control and Civil Air Traffic Control Operations**

Integration of joint airspace control and civil ATC is vital to successful joint/multinational air operations. **The ACP should provide procedures to fully integrate the resources of the military and civil ATC facilities responsible for terminal-area airspace control or en route ATC when required.** Civil ATC integration may require detailed negotiations through the Department of State or national and local ATC agencies. All ATC elements or their liaisons should be involved from the outset in planning and executing airspace management and should make sure airspace requirements get coordinated with and approved by the appropriate agencies. Elements may need to participate in the development and integration of an HN airspace infrastructure. ATC personnel may also provide planning, terminal, airspace information, and forward-area support services to aviation assets conducting nation assistance.

5. **Integration of Joint Airspace Control and Air Defense Operations**

Integration of joint airspace control and air defense is also vital to successful joint/multinational air operations.

a. **Prioritization and integration of joint airspace control and air defense activities is essential.** Airspace control procedures will be used to assist in aircraft identification, facilitate engagement of enemy aircraft, and provide safe passage of friendly aircraft.

b. **ROE and procedures must give air defense forces freedom to engage manned and unmanned hostile aircraft and missiles.** However, procedures must be established in the ACP and promulgated in the ACO to allow identification of friendly aircraft, to prevent delays in offensive operations, and mitigate situations which could cause fratricide. These **procedures need to be simple to execute for both aircrews and surface air defense personnel** and may include visual, electronic, geographic, and/or maneuver means for sorting friend from foe. Air defense operations should not cause delays in air operations by creating unnecessarily complicated or lengthy air route structures. ACMs should not unduly restrain surface-to-air weapons. Airspace control procedures objectives are shown in Figure III-3.

c. Air defense forces and systems are vulnerable to massed attacks across narrow frontages, therefore a flexible and adaptable ACP with well thought out airspace control procedures is essential to providing the JFC freedom of maneuver within the operational area. The procedures should allow coordinated employment of air, land, or maritime air defense systems against the threat, and use the inherent flexibility of air defense airborne platforms to mass forces to meet the enemy attackers.

AIRSPACE CONTROL PROCEDURES OBJECTIVES

- Enhance effectiveness in accomplishing the joint force commander's objectives.
- Facilitate air defense identification.
- Prevent mutual interference.
- Prevent fratricide.
- Safely accommodate and expedite the flow of all air traffic in the operational area.

Figure III-3. Airspace Control Procedures Objectives

6. **Airspace Integration and Joint Fires**

a. Airspace control procedures increase in complexity and detail when air forces operate in proximity to, or in conjunction with, surface forces. **Liaison elements are vital when integrating air and surface elements in close proximity.** Each area of operations (AO) may be defined with specific boundaries. Within each AO there are typically maneuver control measures such as boundaries, FSCMs, fire support coordination line (FSCL), ACMs, or multiples of these measures.

b. **Close coordination is required to deconflict and integrate airspace use with the employment of joint fires.** Component fire support agencies establish FSCMs. Deconfliction of airspace and joint fires normally occurs during mission planning and FSCMs and ACMs are disseminated through command and fire support channels. Real-time coordination, deconfliction, and integration of airspace and joint fires with airspace control agencies and C2 nodes are essential in fluid situations.

c. **ACMs are employed to facilitate the efficient use of airspace to accomplish missions and simultaneously provide safeguards for friendly forces.** Examples include restricted operation areas, air-to-air refueling area (AAR), and corridors. ACMs provide the three-dimensional description of the airspace, associated restrictions, requests for access, and other applicable coordination procedures. The ACP should specify the categories of ACMs in use for the JOA along with coordination and promulgation methods. The ACP also should include FSCMs and any coalition or HN ACMs in use.

d. The coordinating altitude (CA) is an ACM. It uses altitude to separate users and as the transition between different airspace coordinating entities. Examples of airspace coordinating entities include command and reporting center, air support operations center, Airborne Warning and Control System, E-2C, air traffic service, Joint Surveillance Target Attack Radar System, air defense artillery, Marine tactical air command center, direct air support center, or Army corps/division airspace C2 element, air defense airspace management/brigade airspace element, etc. The airspace coordinating entities should be included in the ACP and promulgated in the ACO. Army echelons incorporate ACP guidance and integrate the ACO, AADP, SPINS, and ATO via operations orders. All airspace users should coordinate with the appropriate airspace coordinating entities when transitioning through or firing through the CA.

e. FSCMs are employed by land or amphibious commanders to facilitate the rapid engagement of targets and simultaneously provide safeguards for friendly forces. FSCMs are usually activated for a limited time and refer to areas where fires may be permitted or restricted.

f. The requirement to integrate airspace use in support of ground fire missions requires the determination of the firing locations, the impact location, and the airspace that will be transited by the projectile during flight. Those projectile parameters are integrated with other airspace users. Service liaisons and airspace control agencies work closely to ensure that appropriate ACMs and FSCMs integrate surface operations and airspace operations. See JP 3-09, *Joint Fire Support,* for further details.

7. Methods of Joint Airspace Control

The methods of airspace control vary across the range of military operations. They range from positive control of all air assets in an airspace control area to procedural control of all such assets, or any effective combination of the two. ACPs and systems need to accommodate these methods based on component, joint, and national capabilities and requirements. Positive control relies on radars, other sensors, cooperative identification systems (IFF/selective identification feature [SIF], precise participant location and identification, blue force tracker, etc.), digital data links, and other elements of the air defense system to positively identify, track, and direct air assets. Procedural control relies on ACMs, such as comprehensive air defense identification procedures and ROE, low-level transit routes (LLTRs), minimum-risk routes (MRRs), aircraft identification maneuvers, FSCMs, CAs, ROZs, restricted fire areas, free fire areas, no fire areas, standard use Army aircraft flight routes (SAAFRs), and high-density airspace control zones (HIDACZs). Procedural ACMs for UAS, Army Tactical Missile Systems (ATACMS), Global Positioning System Multiple Launch Rocket System (GMLRS), Tomahawk land attack missiles (TLAMs), and other cruise missile systems include special corridors, surface-to-surface missile system measures, restricted operations areas, and altitude reservations. Figure III-4 summarizes positive and procedural methods of airspace control. A list of ACMs with accompanying descriptions, discussion of uses, and considerations is contained in Appendix B, "Airspace Coordinating and Fire Support Coordination Measures." **The airspace control structure needs to be responsive to evolving enemy threat conditions and changing tactical situations.** Enemy forces will attempt to degrade airspace control capabilities by direct attack and electronic measures.

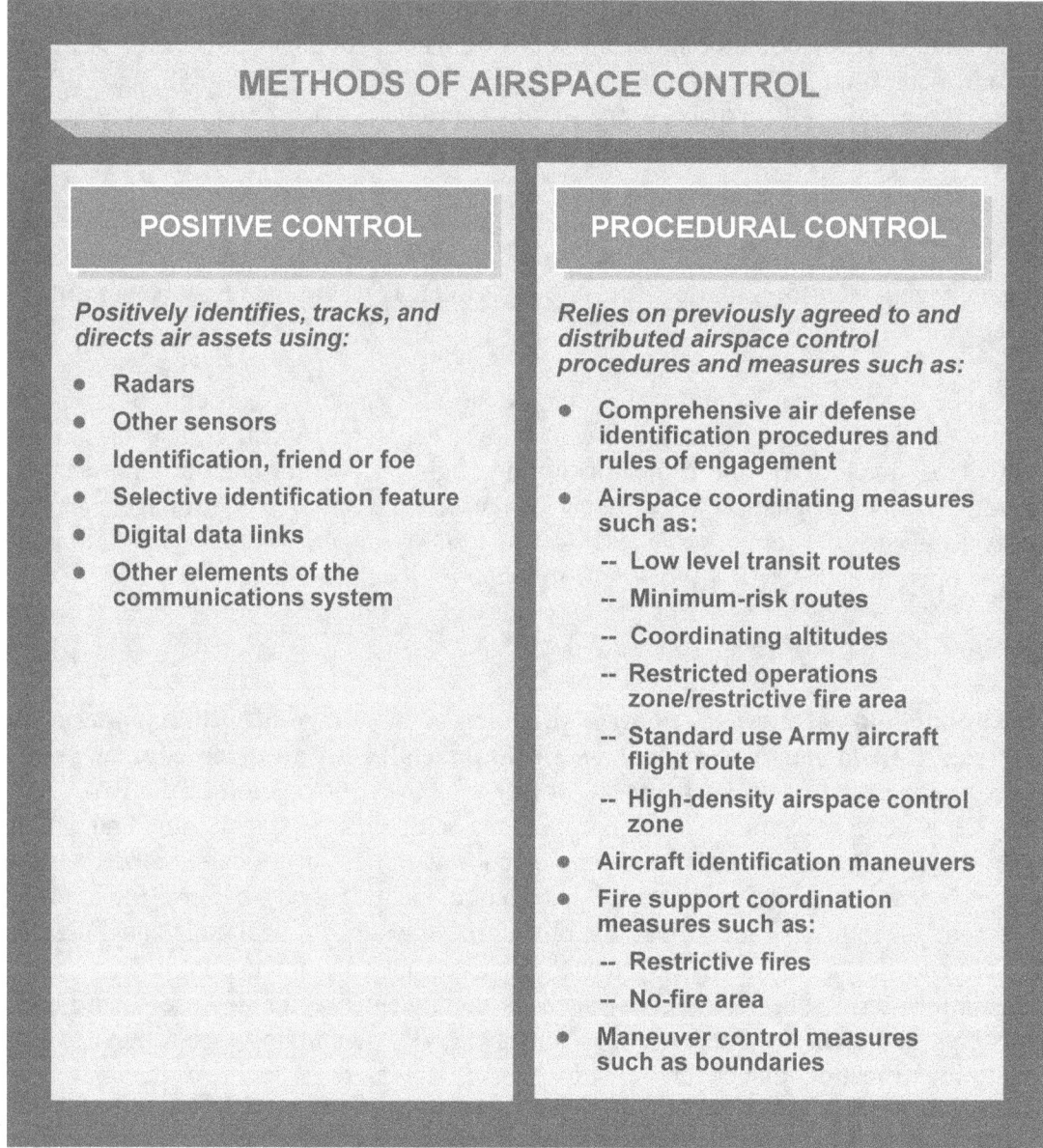

Figure III-4. Methods of Airspace Control

8. **Enemy Air Engagement Operations**

    Engaging enemy aircraft with friendly air, land, and maritime assets must be fully coordinated to optimize all aspects of friendly combat power. This reduces uncoordinated simultaneous engagements, unengaged penetrators, and fratricide.

    a. **Joint Engagement Zone (JEZ) Operations.** These operations involve the employment and integration of multiple air defense systems in order to simultaneously engage enemy targets in the operational area. Targets within the JEZ may be prioritized for engagement based on friendly weapons system strengths; for example, fighters could be designated to primarily engage enemy aircraft, while concurrently, surface-based missiles would be designated to primarily engage enemy missile threats in the same zone.

However, **successful JEZ operations depend on positively identifying friendly, neutral, and enemy aircraft.** Positive control may ensure that real-time engagement taskings are based on comprehensive situational awareness. Under procedural control, all air defense systems must be capable of accurately discerning between enemy, neutral, and friendly aircraft in a highly complex environment before full joint engagement operations can occur. If these conditions cannot be met, separate zones for missile and fighter engagement should be established. **JEZ operations require effective C2.** Positive control is normally used within a JEZ during maritime operations.

b. **Fighter Engagement Zone (FEZ) Operations. These operations usually take place above and beyond the range of surface-based (land and sea) air defenses.** Effective FEZ operations are highly dependent on coordination and flexibility within the ACS. **FEZ operations enable the JFC to respond immediately with fighter assets** to an enemy air offensive regardless of its location. FEZ and missile engagement zone (MEZ) operations present the enemy with the dilemma of defending against two entirely different weapon systems, greatly decreasing enemy survivability. FEZ operations within the airspace control area should not result in undue restraints on the ability of surface-based air defense systems to engage the threat.

c. **MEZ Operations.** These operations are ideal for point defense of critical assets, protection of maneuver units in the forward area, and area coverage of the joint security area. **MEZ operations offer the JFC the ability to engage the enemy with a high- and low-altitude, all-weather capability.** Advanced surface-to-air missile systems have long-range, high-firepower capability that can engage enemy aircraft beyond the forward line of own troops (FLOT) or disrupt massed enemy air attacks prior to committing fighter assets. Properly employed, **MEZ operations are effective across the full range of air defense operations and enemy threats. MEZ operations need to be designed to maximize the full range and capabilities of various systems.** MEZ operations within the airspace control area should not result in undue restraints on the flexibility and ability of friendly air assets to respond to changing threats.

d. **Coordination for Engagement Operations.** The following general guidelines apply for coordination of engagement operations:

(1) For urgent or emergency combat situations, **the ACA can authorize deviations from established policies and procedures.** In these situations, the ACA should notify all affected air defense assets and airspace users prior to authorizing deviations. The JFC should be informed as soon as possible.

(2) When the circumstances necessitate the rapid deployment and employment of forces for which there are no approved OPLANs or previously established ACPs, **a temporary ACS** responsive to immediate tactical or operational requirements will be established.

e. **Airspace Control and Integration of Friendly EW and Suppression of Enemy Air Defenses (SEAD). The JFC integrates EW and SEAD into the overall planning**

effort, and an EW coordination cell may be established to perform this function. Proper integration of EW can help prevent degrading the effectiveness of airspace control assets and ensure the positive control aspects of the system. Failure to integrate EW may degrade the effectiveness of some airspace control assets, degrade some of the positive control aspects of the system, reduce the capability to identify aircraft, and require increased dependence on coordination through procedural control measures. Additional procedural control measures may also be required to compensate for foreseen degradations that cannot be avoided. Thorough planning is required to preclude EW and SEAD efforts from unduly degrading air defense and airspace control efforts.

9. **Multinational Integration Issues**

International agreements, enemy and friendly force structures, commanders' CONOPS, and the operational environment will determine specific arrangements for airspace control while conducting multinational operations. **Effective coordination between all multinational forces is essential to mission success and to avoid fratricide.** All multinational aircraft involved in the operation should appear on the daily ATO to help ensure deconfliction and effective airspace control.

See JP 3-16, Multinational Operations, *and Allied Joint Publication 3.3.5(A),* Doctrine for Joint Airspace Control, *for more information regarding the responsibilities and requirements of ACSs during multinational operations.*

10. **Unmanned Aircraft**

a. UA may be operated in the airspace control area by each joint force component, multinational forces, and other government agencies. **The established principles of airspace management used in manned flight operations will normally apply to UA operations.** However, UA may be difficult to visually acquire and do not always provide a clear radar or electronic signature, presenting a potential hazard to other aircraft. Therefore, UA operations require special considerations in terms of airspace control and usage. Specific UA volumes of airspace may need to be included in the ACO. Additionally, the ACO should provide times of activation of airspace for UA operations. In cases where a standing ACO is used, specific details will be addressed in the ATO/SPINS. In either case, efforts should be made to integrate UA with manned flight operations to enable a more flexible and adaptable airspace structure.

b. While the C2 processes for UA are similar to those for manned assets, several characteristics of UA can make C2 particularly challenging:

(1) UAS communication links are generally more critical than those required for manned systems. In the event of lost communications, a manned aircraft will typically press with the mission and/or return safely to a home base or alternate field. However, UA rely on a nearly continuous stream of communication (for both flight control and payload) to successfully complete a mission. Therefore, communications security, and specifically bandwidth protection (from both friendly interference and

adversary action), is imperative. Although UA may be capable of autonomous reaction (i.e., collision avoidance) or preplanned response in the event of lost communication (i.e., return to base), they typically rely on a near-continuous data exchange for both flight control and payload management. Accordingly, airspace planners must account for these contingencies.

(2) UA may be capable of transferring control of the aircraft and/or payloads to multiple operators while airborne. Close coordination amongst all potential operators is required. Additionally, specific communications-outage procedures should be clearly defined in the event communications are lost or jammed entirely.

(3) Current UA are typically not as robust as manned systems when component failures or environmental extremes are encountered. Wind, precipitation, turbulence, and icing can significantly degrade or altogether nullify UA platform and/or sensor capabilities.

(4) Most larger UA have considerably longer endurance times than comparable manned systems. Planners must exploit this capability when tasking UA assets.

c. Defensive Considerations. Our adversaries are developing and acquiring UA so it is imperative for our C2 and DCA nodes to be able to differentiate between friendly and enemy UA and cruise missiles. The ACP must not allow a window of opportunity for adversaries to exploit. Specifically, the use of CA and SAAFR by UA enables efficient and timely use of the airspace, but also makes it more difficult for air defense operators to differentiate between friend and foe. This type of airspace control is typically procedural control, and not positive control. Therefore, UAS operators must follow prescribed airspace control procedures and air defense identification procedures in order to prevent fratricide and/or prevent enemy UA exploitation of that airspace.

For a more detailed discussion of UA considerations, see Field Manual (FM) 3-04.15/Navy Tactics, Techniques, and Procedures (NTTP) 3-55.14/Air Force Tactics, Techniques, and Procedures (Instruction) (AFTTP[I]) 3-2.64 Multi-Service Tactics, Techniques, and Procedures for the Tactical Employment of Unmanned Aircraft Systems.

11. Theater Missiles

Theater missiles (e.g., conventional air launched cruise missiles, ATACMS, GMLRS, and TLAM) are standoff weapons fired from a launch point on a preprogrammed flight profile to a designated target. Because these missiles have a small radar cross-section, they are difficult to track with normal radar units conducting airspace control. Therefore, positive control is not an effective means to deconflict theater missile operations from other air operations. **It is imperative that procedural ACMs be established in the ATO, ACO, or SPINS.** Procedural ACMs for theater missiles may include ROZs for launch and target locations, missile flight path, corridors, which include specified altitudes and position area hazard/target area hazard locations for ATACMS.

12. Airspace Control in Maritime Operations

a. In **joint maritime operations,** specific control and defensive measures may differ from those used in a land-based operation. The joint force maritime component commander (JFMCC) may be designated the control authority for a specific airspace control area or sector for the accomplishment of a specific mission. The massing of maritime forces into a strike force of combined arms (air, surface, and subsurface) under a single commander reduces the front to be defended, enhances mutual support, and simplifies identification and deconfliction of friendly aircraft and other air defense measures. To ensure unity of effort and minimal interference along adjacent boundaries, **the commander responsible for maritime airspace control must coordinate with the ACA.**

b. In joint operations composed of **adjacent maritime and land environments,** specific control and defensive measures may be a composite of those measures normally employed in each environment. **The JFC for such operations needs to ensure detailed coordination of control and defensive measures with the affected air, land, and maritime component commanders.** Additionally:

(1) Assignment of airspace allows the JFC to exercise C2 of forces, deconflict high volumes of aircraft and missiles, and defend forces. During amphibious operations, JFMCC or the commander, amphibious task force (ATF), is normally designated as the control authority. The complexity and size of an amphibious operation directly determines the amount of airspace allocated.

(2) The level of airspace control allocated to the amphibious force depends on the type of ACM approved for the operation. If an AOA is established, air control procedures are identical to HIDACZ procedures. **If only an AO is established, the amphibious force will normally request that the ACA establish a HIDACZ over this geographic area.** A HIDACZ is airspace designated in an ACP or ACO in which there is a concentrated employment of numerous and varied weapons and airspace users. Access is normally controlled by the maneuver commander who can direct a more restrictive weapons status within the designated area. For air defense, the amphibious defense zone includes the AOA plus a buffer zone so that the incoming threat can be engaged before it crosses into the AOA. The items shown below should be considered when establishing a HIDACZ:

(a) Airspace control capabilities of the maritime force.

(b) Procedures for expeditious movement of aircraft into and out of the HIDACZ.

(c) Range and type of naval surface fire support available.

(d) Coordination of fire support, as well as air defense weapons control orders or status within and in the vicinity of the HIDACZ.

(e) Entry and exit routes and procedures into and out of the HIDACZ and to the target area.

(f) Air traffic advisory as required. Procedures and systems must also be considered for ATC service during instrument meteorological conditions.

(g) Location of enemy forces inside and in close proximity to the HIDACZ.

(h) At a minimum, the HIDACZ should cover the ATF sea echelon areas and extend inland to the landing force's FSCL. Additionally, the HIDACZ should be large enough to accommodate the flow of fixed-wing aircraft into and out of the amphibious airspace.

(3) Under the ATF, the Navy tactical air control center is normally the agency responsible for controlling all air operations within the allocated airspace regardless of mission or origin, to include supporting arms. An airborne element or surface combatant with the requisite air C2 capabilities may also serve this function. Regardless of where actual airspace control is exercised, close and continuous coordination between airspace control and air defense agencies is essential in any amphibious operation. Emphasis will be placed on simple, flexible ATC plans and a combination of positive and procedural airspace control. Most amphibious operations will take place in a radar environment, allowing for increased control over air missions. Amphibious forces operating in a non-radar environment will rely exclusively on procedural control. Amphibious air control plans employ a combination of positive and procedural control methods.

For further details on airspace control in amphibious operations, refer to JP 3-02, Amphibious Operations.

c. Considerations need to be made for aircraft based outside the AO. There is a good probability that aircraft will have to transit carrier control zones. Corridors can be preplanned, limiting impact on carrier operations. Corridors should be planned to minimize aircraft flight time/fuel requirements.

13. High-Density Airspace Control Zone Integration with Other Airspace Coordinating Measures

In some cases, the operational environment may require an airspace/fires density level that exceeds the capability of a single HIDACZ controlling authority. One method to prevent overloading the controlling authority is to establish another ACM (restricted operations area, HIDACZ, etc.) above or adjacent to the HIDACZ, controlled by another agency or component.

For more information on HIDACZ, see FM 3-52.1/Air Force Tactics, Techniques, and Procedures (AFTTP) 3-2.78, Multi-Service Tactics, Techniques, and Procedures for Airspace Control.

Intentionally Blank

CHAPTER IV
AIRSPACE CONTROL EXECUTION BY PHASE

"The way of the warrior is to master the virtue of his weapons."

Miyamato Musashi, *A Book of Five Rings*

The JP 5-0, *Joint Operation Planning,* phasing construct is an extremely useful guide to generalize airspace control responsibilities, activities, systems, documents, and liaison requirements across the range of military operations. Although an operation could proceed logically from phase 0 to V, most operations will not. Each operation is unique and will require unique solutions to military obstacles.

1. **Phase 0 — Shape**

a. The shape phase is inclusive of normal and routine military airspace activities to deter potential adversaries and ensure or solidify relationships with friends and allies. Various joint, multinational, and interagency airspace activities are executed with the intent to enhance international legitimacy and gain cooperation in support of defined military and national strategic objectives. They are designed to ensure success by shaping perceptions and influencing the behavior of both adversaries and allies, developing allied and friendly military capabilities for self-defense and coalition operations, improving information exchange and intelligence sharing, and providing US forces with peacetime and contingency airspace access.

b. **The HN retains ACA and joint forces primarily use existing international or HN aeronautical information publications (AIPs) for airspace procedures or guidelines**; airspace and navigation services are the sovereign right and responsibility of the HN.

c. **Although the JFC may not designate a standing ACA during this phase, the JFC should appoint a lead agent, normally the commander, Air Force forces, for coordinating the resolution of issues related to airspace management, ATC, terminal instrument procedures, and navigation aids within the operational area.** The commander, Navy forces, is normally assigned responsibility for airspace procedures applicable to fleet air operations over international waters within the operational area and only advises the JFC's lead agent as appropriate. The JFC's lead agent is delegated the authority for developing joint force airspace requirements in coordination with the other Service components and representing those joint force airspace requirements to the Department of Defense (DOD), interagency, international, or HN authorities as appropriate. Additionally, the lead agent normally serves as the focal point to:

(1) Provide assistance to the JFC, components, Services, and supporting commands on airspace, air traffic, or navigation aid matters.

(2) Develop appropriate ACMs in support of JFC contingency planning to include airspace requirements for UA.

(3) Ensure current and future airspace and navigation aid availability for components and supporting commands through joint mission essential task listing inputs.

(4) Coordinate HN navigation aids inspections with US Air Force Flight Standards Agency, US Army Air Traffic Services Command, Headquarters US Army, United States Army Aeronautical Services Agency, Federal Aviation Administration (FAA)/ICAO aviation system standards, and the DOD program management office for flight inspection.

(5) Ensure navigation aids are included on the DOD essential foreign-owned navigation aids list if deemed an enduring requirement.

(6) Develop and establish procedures for airspace actions or issues that cannot be resolved by component commands consistent with applicable DOD, JFC, component, international, and HN guidance.

(7) Ensure altitude reservations are coordinated for all DOD aircraft transiting or operating within the operational area.

(8) Develop friendly HN airspace capabilities through the joint force theater engagement plan, training, and exercises.

d. In addition to ensuring continuation of routine DOD flight operations during the shaping phase, joint force airspace planners establish effective relationships with key operational area airspace authorities, develop specific ACPs in preparation for future operations, and build airspace planning expertise. Regular DOD or joint force interaction with HN authorities and participation in regional airspace conferences establishes relationships with the HN for quick resolution of issues and effective coordination of airspace requirements.

e. Development of ACPs should be as thorough as possible and include airspace control considerations from peace to combat operations and through all follow-on phases of the OPLAN. Additionally, **the ACP should integrate known international or HN air traffic airspace and air defense capabilities.** Primary planning considerations include identification of airspace required for joint force operations and proposed coordination process for obtaining that airspace. Joint operation planning should consider procedures to transfer ACS from the HN to the ACA, rerouting of airways, ACA responsibilities to continuity of civil aviation operations, and HN notification of ACA areas of control through notices to airmen (NOTAMs) or AIP entries. Appendix A, "Airspace Control Plan Development Considerations," illustrates the ACP development process.

f. Special consideration should be given to planning airspace management responses to long-range missile launches into friendly territory. Rapid notification procedures should be developed and practiced to allow unhindered rapid response to defeating enemy missiles in flight.

2. Phase I — Deter

a. Transition to phase I begins with identification and determination of a crisis situation requiring joint force action and crisis action planning to develop a campaign plan with ACP if no OPLAN or concept plan exists. Available joint force airspace planners will develop or revise the ACP for airspace actions required in phase I execution as well as considerations and planning for follow-on phases.

b. Strategic Considerations. Upon receipt of authoritative planning direction, airspace planning must be refined to reflect and support the planning effort in light of the situation. Airspace planning necessarily entails coordination with international and multiple national authorities and is politically sensitive. Release of airspace plans can potentially compromise OPSEC, but can also increase the geographic uncertainty of potential adversaries and may have deterrent or deceptive effects. Since the airspace planning and preparation measures discussed in the following paragraphs may also have the same effects, airspace planning and coordination efforts must be considered with other strategic undertakings.

c. The deter phase is normally a demonstration of joint force capabilities and resolve to deter undesirable adversary action. It is largely characterized by preparatory actions that specifically facilitate execution of subsequent phases of the operation or theater campaign. Specific airspace actions may include developing the finalized ACP and airspace database build for ACO publication; obtaining initial over flight and airspace permission; and assignment of joint force airspace liaison personnel to Department of State, US embassies, multinational, or HN organizations to coordinate airspace requirements for subsequent phases of the operation. **Liaisons can facilitate timely exchange of airspace control information,** especially in a multinational environment where language barriers can impede crucial cross-communication necessary for safe and effective airspace control.

d. The ACA (or JFC's lead agent for airspace management) establishes a dedicated airspace planning team to finalize the ACP, coordinate with the AADC for AADP deconfliction, and develop the ACO for current and future operations. **The ACP and AADP should complement each other and ensure the orderly transition from peacetime operations to combat operations.** The ACA (lead agent) may:

(1) Coordinate with the JFC, components, interagency, coalition, and HN to define airspace boundaries for inclusion in the ACP (if granted liaison authority from the JFC).

(2) Request airspace planning augmentation from components, Services, interagency or multinational organizations as required for planning efforts and/or as liaisons.

(3) Establish key relationships or agreements with appropriate international and regional airspace control agencies concerning ACA and coordination during joint force operations.

(4) Identify required joint force ACSs and personnel required to support airspace control through phased operations and deploy those assets as required.

(5) Coordinate DOD/FAA/ICAO NOTAM system availability to support intertheater dissemination of flight operating information, flight check aircraft, and scheduling for air traffic facility inspection.

(6) Identify the desired concept for the ACSs in phase IV/V and consider placing critical components of the enemy air control system on the restricted target list to preserve them for future use.

e. For the deter phase, **the ACP should contain procedures to fully integrate the resources of military and civil ATC facilities responsible for terminal-area airspace control or en route ATC.** Airspace management personnel should coordinate the ACP with representatives of the HN in whose airspace the operations will take place and with civil air activities that may occur in or near the airspace. Broad areas of concern for developing the ACP include familiarity with the basic OPLAN, knowledge of host and multinational capabilities, procedures of military and civil airspace control and ATC systems, and general locations of friendly and enemy forces.

f. Additionally, any HN agreements that could impact air operations must be considered. HN agreements concerning airspace control may only be negotiated by authorized personnel in accordance with DOD instructions and ICAO protocols. Surface-to-air weapons and air defense aircraft should be integrated for maximum effectiveness. **Proper coordination with civil air operations is especially important during transitions into or out of wartime status or during non-wartime periods of heightened tensions.** Political constraints, national and military ACSs and procedures, and the capabilities and limitations of these systems are important considerations in planning for required joint force airspace control. Applicable information from the ACP should be distributed to joint and coalition forces as well as HNs, allies, and international organizations such as ICAO.

3. **Phase II — Seize the Initiative**

a. Transition to phase II may be accomplished on the JFC's initiative or in response to an enemy attack. During combat operations, peacetime airspace rules and organizations change, and the nature of these changes will vary from theater to theater. **The ACP should contain instructions to transition from peacetime to combat in**

simple, clear steps. The ACP should include the airspace control concepts for transition to phase II operations and robust control methods for potential degraded operations. Airspace planners should be integrated into development of the master air attack plan to ensure required airspace is designed for combat operations and the transition from peacetime to combat airspace control is seamless.

b. At the outset of phase II combat operations **every effort should be made to exclude civil aviation operations from the affected JOA.** Redesign of airspace or notification of impending changes to airspace control could signal adversaries of a pending operation so timing for airspace transition to potential combat should be considered. Advanced or open notification of airspace changes should be integrated into the information OPLAN for OPSEC or tactical deception considerations.

c. **Joint air operations play a critical role in actions to seize the initiative or gain access to a theater or JOA.** During phase II, the JFC seeks to seize the initiative in combat and noncombat situations through the application of appropriate joint force capabilities. In combat operations this involves executing offensive operations at the earliest appropriate time, forcing the enemy to offensive culmination and setting the conditions for decisive operations. Normally the beginning of phase II signals the shift from peace to combat operations.

d. Integrating the airspace control function with DCA and offensive counterair operations is especially critical during efforts to gain air superiority. Effective identification procedures are required for both airspace control and DCA to facilitate engagement of enemy aircraft and missiles, and provide safe passage of friendly aircraft and missiles.

e. In the opening stages of phase II, effective airspace control hinges on understanding the OPLAN, JFC intent, the airspace environment, and the requirements to effectively control it. The JFACC will publish the AOD which describes the JFACC's implementation of JFC intent and provides guidance for operations prioritization. **During major operations the JFACC is typically the supported commander for the counterair effort in the operational area and integrates offensive and DCA to achieve air superiority.** Against adversaries with a credible air and air defense threat, efforts to "seize the initiative" will likely be more sequential than simultaneous because many operations may require air superiority as a precondition for success. For phase II operations where the US already has access and air superiority, the ACP and the AADP may be less restrictive, and operations to establish the required access may be either sequential or simultaneous.

f. Until air superiority is achieved, the phase II ACP may restrict friendly military and civil airspace users. **Operating platforms with limited identification and communications equipment places those systems at risk and also complicates counterair operations by increasing the risk of fratricide and the probability of successful enemy air or missile attacks.** Certain friendly airborne systems (cruise missiles, UA) may be mission-essential and yet lack identification, communications equipment, or autonomous sense-and-avoid capability. Specific ACMs are required for these users to minimize the impact to the counterair fight while maximizing efforts to seize the initiative. **Systems that cannot be positively identified as friendly may be restricted during the opening stages of combat operations prior to obtaining air superiority.** At commencement of combat operations the JFACC should immediately execute plans and procedures to reduce civil aviation to levels most compatible with combat operations. Some level of civil aviation, especially commercial airlift flying in support of coalition operations, will probably be ongoing throughout all the phases.

g. The JFACC should ensure the ACP and ACO are fully coordinated with supporting components, coalition partners, and HN air and air defense forces, even if the HN is not participating in combat operations. This coordination should also include all SOF elements that participate in the phase II access operations. Because some of these plans are highly sensitive, the JFACC should ensure alternate communication means are available to pass information to friendly organizations that do not have access to normal military communications.

h. Phase II airspace control planning should fully integrate fires from all friendly and coalition forces. **Failure to integrate all fires in initial planning significantly increases the potential for fratricide and may delay execution of combat operations.** Early integration of airspace and fires prevents costly decisions which result when two components plan to use the same airspace, at the same time, for different missions.

i. **The JFACC, working with the JFC and other components, should clearly identify the risk of combining fires and aircraft operations** (manned and unmanned), particularly at the outset of the campaign when airspace may be more constrained due to the higher density of air and land operations. These risks should be codified in the ACP, along with the level of risk the JFC is willing to accept for each phase.

j. Component fires systems, such as conventional air-launched cruise missile, TLAM, ATACMS, and other systems, have small radar cross sections and are difficult to track with typical air control radar systems. In addition, most of these systems are uncontrolled once they are fired or launched. They should be deconflicted with procedural ACMs. The ACP should establish procedures to include procedural control and coordination of fires. These procedures should also include real-time deconfliction measures for missions in the ATO, ACO, and SPINS.

k. **The JFACC normally serves as the supported commander for the JFC's overall air interdiction effort.** Airspace control, to include integration with fires, is critical to the success of air interdiction. The JFACC should ensure that all air interdiction operations use common reference systems and tactics, techniques, and procedures (TTP). The JFACC advises the JFC and includes the coordinated common reference systems and TTP in the ACP, AADP, ATO, ACO, and SPINS. These plans should also include real-time airspace control procedures for the engagement of time-sensitive targets.

l. The use of UA over the battlefield has increased significantly in recent years. UA require access to airspace with manned aircraft, particularly in the vicinity of high value targets. In order to minimize risk and maximize the effectiveness of UA, **the ACP should direct the deconfliction of joint, component, and coalition UA platforms.** Unlike their manned counterparts, the vast majority of UA do not have on-board sense-and-avoid capabilities. Therefore, other means of aircraft separation must be employed to reduce the risk of mid-air collisions. UA deconfliction is critical during all phases of an operation and requires detailed planning and coordination.

m. During phase II the JFC and the components should conduct thorough intelligence preparation of the battlespace as part of the joint intelligence preparation of the operational environment. Part of this intelligence preparation includes information gained through the use of ISR platforms. Many ISR platforms are airspace users and may require access to the same airspace. **Prior to the JFACC achieving air superiority, friendly airborne ISR platforms that do not meet identification or control requirements increase the difficulty of counterair operations and increase the risk of successful enemy air attack.** If the JFC decides to restrict the use of friendly platforms without sufficient identification or communications systems, the ACP should clearly delineate which operating areas are restricted, and what capabilities (e.g., IFF) are required to operate within them. If the JFC elects not to restrict operations by these systems, the ACA should clearly outline the increased risk to the JFC for approval.

n. ISR asset airspace congestion over high interest areas may be mitigated through an effective and integrated airborne ISR collection plan. In addition, the ability to disseminate ISR products rapidly across the strategic, operational, and tactical levels (Remote Operations Video Enhanced Receiver [ROVER] down-link, for example) may decrease airspace congestion. **Multiple, component-organic, airborne ISR assets staring at the same objective area add complexity to airspace control operations and may delay fire support to forces on the ground.** For more information, see JP 2-0, *Joint Intelligence.*

o. Regardless of whether the operation or campaign is sequential or simultaneous, the joint force land component commander (JFLCC), if designated, or one or more land component commanders will normally become the supported commanders for their AOs during the latter stages of phase II. Ideally, the air component will have achieved at least localized air superiority over the AO; however, this may not always be the case. Once air superiority is achieved, the JFC may allow increased operations by airborne systems with limited identification and communications capabilities. An area-wide COP with minimum latency is a significant contributor to both air defense and airspace control. **The ACP may employ fewer restrictions on certain systems which are visible on the airspace COP, whereas systems with less identification and communications equipment may require more restrictions and coordination.**

p. When one or more land component commanders become supported commanders for their AOs, the ACS should be modified and integrated to meet mission requirements.

The ACA should consider the following when creating the phase II transition portion of the ACP:

(1) The C2 plan for the initial employment of ground forces.

(2) Adequate communications within the operational area to execute the plan.

(3) ACS elements required to meet the scheme of maneuver for component commanders.

(4) Delegation of ACA to components (e.g., joint special operations area, AOA, HIDACZ, or sectors) and integration of component airspace control agencies.

(5) Planned use of adversary systems for the post-hostility ACS (consider which, if any, facilities should be placed on the restricted target list for preservation).

q. **A key role of the ACP is to define the processes to propose, approve, modify, and promulgate ACMs and FSCMs.** The ACA establishes ACMs with components and coalition airspace users and provides recommended airspace control procedures for JFC approval and publication in the ACP. Once approved, these ACP ACMs are promulgated throughout the joint and coalition forces via the ACO, ATO, and SPINS. For effective airspace control it is critical that all joint and multinational airspace users, including indirect fires platforms, understand the area-wide ACMs including:

(1) Activation of FSCMs including FSCL, kill box, etc.

(2) Establishment of the CA if used.

(3) ACMs required for special missions (e.g., air assaults, airborne operations).

(4) Areas that will become high density airspace and the type of control procedures used to mitigate risk.

(5) Automated tools and systems that ensure promulgation of the ACO and changes to airspace users.

4. **Phase III — Dominate**

a. Phase III includes the full employment of joint force capabilities and continues the appropriate sequencing of forces into the operational area as quickly as possible. When an operation or campaign is focused on conventional enemy forces, the "dominate" phase normally concludes with decisive operations that drive an enemy to culmination and achieve the JFC's operational objectives. During major operations, phase III may involve ground forces and require bringing a large number of manned and unmanned aircraft into the operational area. In addition, the amount of fires assets using airspace will likely increase, requiring additional planning, deconfliction, and airspace control actions. The ACP should include updates and changes that will occur as the JFC transitions the force to phase III.

b. During phase III operations, the ACP/ATO/ACO and SPINS should be updated to include responsibilities and authorities (including SOF and coalition) for the following:

(1) Designated areas within JFLCC/JFMCC AOs.

(2) Procedures for forward operating bases (FOBs) and airfields.

(3) ATC/air traffic service at FOBs.

(4) ATC/air traffic service at captured airfields.

(5) Area air defense and short-range air defense integration behind the FSCL and FLOT.

(6) Fixed wing, UA, and rotary wing deconfliction methods.

c. During phase III, airspace control elements should expect a significant increase in the number of indirect fires in the JFLCC/JFMCC AO. Indirect fire systems are airspace users; however, current airspace control TTP and FSCMs do not lend themselves to seamless integration. ACMs do not normally prevent fires from entering the airspace; only FSCMs serve to restrict fires. **To effectively integrate fires and airspace control, airspace control elements should determine which ACMs must also be protected by an airspace coordination area or air corridor and coordinate accordingly.** As an example, an AAR is an ACM which would prevent other aircraft from entering the area without coordination with the controlling agency. Without an airspace coordination area or air corridor, however, **nothing prevents fires from passing through the AAR.** Integrating fires with other airspace users requires careful consideration of risk and user priority as well as an understanding of the joint air operations plan (JAOP) and land component fires plan.

d. Airspace planners should minimize the number of combined ACM/FSCM requests so as not to overly restrict fires. In the same manner, fires planners should understand there are some areas in which the JFC cannot accept the risk of mixing fires and manned aircraft. Effective real-time execution can solve many of these issues by moving either fires or aircraft to allow both systems to operate. Deconfliction of fires and aircraft is a critical part of phase III airspace control planning.

e. **Missions such as air assaults, airborne assaults, and other incursions into enemy territory require specific airspace control coordination.** These events may require ACMs such as: HIDACZ, ROZ, MRR, or LLTR. These missions may require specific C2 relationships, organizations, and authorities which should be planned for and included in ACP/ATO/ACO and SPINS.

5. Phase IV — Stabilize

a. Phase IV operations ensure that the threat (military or political) is reduced to a manageable level that can be controlled by the potential HN authority and that the situation which led to the original crisis does not recur. During this phase, the joint force may be required to perform local governance until legitimate local entities are functioning. The ACA could be required to perform roles traditionally associated with an HN aviation authority and may include the development of aeronautical information (e.g., instrument procedures, publications, NOTAMs), civil flight planning procedures, certification of procedures, aviation safety investigation, training of HN and/or contract personnel, or operation of airspace infrastructure systems. Considerations should be given to developing aeronautical information to end-state standards expected when control is returned to HN.

b. A key ACA requirement is the development of a plan to establish HN capabilities to effect a successful transfer of airspace control from the joint force to the HN in phase V. The stabilize phase is typically characterized by a change from sustained combat operations to stability operations with increased requests for airspace and airfield access by HN or other non-JFC supporting organizations. **The ACP should address airspace access criteria for non-JFC organizations, joint force to civil airspace priority, and identification and acceptance of associated civil airspace operating risks.** A thorough review of all written guidance should be conducted when the transition to phase IV of operations is anticipated. Documents such as the JAOP, AOD, ACP, AADP, SPINS, ROE, letters of agreement, and international agreements may significantly change in this phase. Priorities for airspace control should be redefined to address increasing civil authority for the airspace environment. Inextricably linked to this review of priorities is a clear determination of what level of risk will be accepted during this phase. The impacts of a catastrophic event involving a civil aircraft could significantly damage the strategic objectives of the JFC and the governments involved in the joint operation. Assistance from the defense attaché office, Department of State, the FAA, ICAO, or a contracted agency should be considered in assisting to establish HN capabilities.

c. **Reducing threats to air operations and establishing security are required to set conditions to transfer airspace control authority to the HN government.** Particularly during this phase, the airspace environment is dynamic and may transition rapidly between varying levels of stability. Throughout this phase, the JFACC continuously balances the needs of military operations against increased civil airspace access and effective transfer of airspace control authority to a legitimate HN entity. **Transition of airspace control to the HN should be considered carefully with regard to continuing JFC military operations.** Reduced military airspace control authority may result in decreased flexibility for operations with increased coordination and approval requirements from the HN. The main transition planning concepts include:

(1) Installation or increased use of commercial systems.

(2) Consolidation and reduction of JFC manpower/systems footprint.

(3) Use of contracted airspace control capabilities.

(4) Joint force ACS linkage to HN systems.

(5) Leveraging HN capabilities and systems.

(6) Transfer of contracts or excess systems to the HN.

(7) Decrease in joint force airspace control support requirements.

(8) Planning to ensure a successful airspace turnover to the HN.

(9) Ensuring required HN capabilities exist.

(10) Developing a clear agreement and timelines for airspace control transfer.

(11) Ensuring continuing joint force airspace mission needs are supported.

d. Interagency coordination and development of an airspace transition plan with key transition milestones are required to reduce friction between the various JFC, USG, international, and HN agencies that may be involved in the airspace transition process. The identification of and agreement on milestone criteria and the airspace infrastructure end state by the various stakeholders are key to a successful transition plan. **Normally, a government or civil organization will handle the planning and requirements for reconstituting the HN ACS.** However, the ACA may be the only one able to assume this primary leadership role especially in seriously degraded or failed state scenarios. The ACA's responsibilities as the acting HN ACA should be detailed in an appropriate delegation document from the HN and referenced in the HN AIP.

e. **The pre-conflict HN airspace control structure (civilian or military controlled) should provide the basic airspace end-state concept unless destroyed or deemed ineffective.** Simplicity and basic effectiveness of the HN airspace system should be a primary goal of the ACA's transition plan. Additionally, the ACA should focus specifically on the ACS to prevent excessive requirements or delays from other aviation-related issues such as airfield construction or certification issues. Also the HN or other supporting agencies may desire to modify or upgrade the ACS which will most likely increase the timelines for the end-state transition milestone. Ideally, the final HN end-state airspace infrastructure plan should meet the minimum requirements for ICAO certification (unless post-conflict situations dictate otherwise) and also take into account HN airspace sovereignty requirements. Interim transfer of airspace control to HN military forces or contracted airspace control services should be considered to allow the redeployment of joint force airspace control forces.

f. **Interoperability between military and civil airspace users and control agencies is crucial** for safe and effective integration of airspace control including air defense, joint fires, and civil aviation. Use of military liaison teams embedded in HN control facilities may be required to ensure the adequate coordination and representation of continuing joint force airspace requirements. Civil documents that govern the HN airspace system may become more authoritative for all airspace users and by the end of phase IV should be the primary source of guidance and regulation. The joint force should ensure that proper agreements exist between the HN and adjacent nations to enable the effective air defense of the country as well as the safe and efficient flow of air traffic across borders. Management and guidance of information assurance and spectrum management should be accounted for in the transition plan. The proliferation of devices that exploit, interrupt, or use the frequency spectrum is likely during this phase as a result of increased activity of other international and HN agencies and general increase in economic communications activities.

g. From an ACA's perspective, the end of phase IV and the beginning of phase V milestone is reached when the framework of the HN ACS is in place and the HN is ready to assume ACA. Phase V is characterized by the processes and events that take place during that transition as joint force personnel and equipment are redeployed and HN personnel and equipment take control.

6. Phase V — Enable Civil Authority

a. This phase is predominantly characterized by joint force support to legitimate civil governance in the operational area. Depending upon the level of indigenous state capacity, joint force activities during phase V may be at the behest of that authority or they may be under its direction. **The joint force will perform key airspace functions either as the delegated ACA or as supporting airspace service provider under the HN aviation authority.** The JFC's ACA can expect frequent coordination and interaction on airspace issues with HN, multinational, interagency, and other airspace system participants. The ACA is in a supporting role to the legitimate civil aviation authority in the region throughout the enable civil authority phase. Normally operations are concluded when joint force redeployment is complete. However, continued joint force support and involvement with the HN and other agencies, beyond the termination of the joint operation, may be required to achieve the desired end state.

b. **Phase V could result as a normal phased transition from phase IV stability operations or as joint force support to a humanitarian relief effort, natural disaster, or other catastrophic event.** During this phase HN aviation regulations and guidance are the authoritative source for airspace control procedures. To the maximum extent possible, original HN aviation and airspace documents should be used by the joint force to comply with HN aviation authority intent. If derivative HN guidance is required for dissemination or amplification in joint force ACP, ACO, ATO, or SPINS, the information should be included verbatim and referenced to the original source document. In situations where HN procedures must be modified by the military for airspace access or use, HN authorities should be consulted and provide appropriate approval of the deviation. Formal agreement or understanding should be coordinated between joint forces and the HN authority to ensure clarity on exact airspace control responsibilities. Frequent and extensive coordination among the joint force, HN, and other agency personnel on airspace control issues may require close proximity of staffs or use of liaisons.

c. Based on the level of required support, **airspace control personnel may be required to provide Service-specific controllers, ACS, liaisons, or trainers to support HN authorities.** JFC and JFACC staff personnel need to ensure that an agreement is in place with the HN authorizing DOD personnel or equipment to provide air traffic services in sovereign HN airspaces. Joint force personnel may be required to use systems provided by the HN or other agencies. Joint force personnel may also be embedded with HN or other agency personnel to provide airspace control services. In these situations, training and certification for joint forces personnel or systems should be determined by the HN authority. Given that few organizations have the deployable airspace control personnel and systems, it should be expected that joint forces support airspace operations using Service ACSs. A combined FAA/Air Force system certification flight check is a unique capability often requested to certify HN radar or navigation aids that have been installed or returned to service. Note: Until acquisition of self-defense capable flight check aircraft, the JFACC may have to orchestrate special procedures (ground patrols in vicinity of approach path, escorts, night-only operations, etc.) to accomplish flight checks in hostile airspace.

d. Setting the conditions and milestones for the relief of joint forces and the reestablishment of effective HN airspace control is crucial for successful phase V termination. HNs with limited capabilities may rely on joint forces for long-term airspace control functions and divert available resources to other higher priority HN programs. In such situations, international, NGO, or contracted services may provide a bridging alternative to take airspace control functions from joint forces until the HN is prepared to accept them.

e. Risk is a fundamental consideration of airspace control. Joint doctrine recognizes the need for each Service and functional component to use the airspace with maximum availability consistent with the JFC acceptable level of risk. **The JFC's acceptable level of risk for all airspace users (including fires) should be clearly delineated in the ACP.** Based on the JFC's guidance, the JFACC develops the AOD to establish the prioritization of operations which may restrict airspace. During all phases the assumption of risk is a command decision. Definitions of high, moderate, and low risk vary from theater to theater based on commander's guidance. In general terms, high risk prioritizes mission accomplishment over the preservation of resources; medium risk seeks to balance mission accomplishment with potential resource losses and may require slight mission adjustments to achieve desired objectives; and low risk prioritizes the preservation of resources and may require substantial mission adjustments to achieve desired objectives. As the volume of airspace users increases, control should be enhanced to keep the level of risk acceptable to the JFC. The ACP should specify areas where high volumes of airspace users are projected and plan for increased control capability. If an enhanced control capability is not an option then commanders should understand they are accepting a higher risk of mid-air collisions and fratricide with indirect fires, manned systems, and UA. Commanders may accept different levels of risk based on the systems involved. For example, a commander may direct that a higher level of risk be accepted for possible fratricide between indirect fires and some or all UA than between indirect fires and manned aircraft.

APPENDIX A
AIRSPACE CONTROL PLAN DEVELOPMENT CONSIDERATIONS

1. **Purpose**

This appendix provides an example of the topics that should be considered when developing an ACP.

2. **Airspace Control Plan Topics**

Every ACP will be different and must be based on the objectives of the military operations, the capabilities and limitations of both friendly and enemy forces, and the contributions and complexities introduced by HN and multinational forces, as well as the access required to the airspace by nonbelligerent aircraft. ACP topics include:

a. Description of the conditions under which the guidance and procedures in the ACP are applicable (e.g., the exercise, OPLAN, OPORD, military operation).

b. Description of the operational area within which the ACP applies.

c. Appointment of the ACA; location of ACA headquarters (HQ) (if required).

d. List of the capabilities that exist within the joint force and in the operational area and that provide airspace control (ground sites, airborne capability) and the means of communicating with those airspace control elements.

e. Description of the duties and responsibilities of:

(1) The ACA.

(2) Each airspace user within the joint force (to include requirements for liaison to and coordination with the ACA).

(3) Each element used in the ACS (site, facility, or airborne platform) and agency specific duties. The plan should delineate whether the agency provides procedural or positive control and its assigned sector.

f. Description of the interface between commanders and coordination elements and the procedures adopted to integrate the ACP with the AADP and deconflict or synchronize airspace requirements for DCA operations and other joint operations.

g. Description of the interface with the FAA, HN ATC system, and/or ICAO.

h. Description of the interface among the theater air control system(s) and the elements within those systems for ATC.

i. If operations include forces from other nations, description of the interfaces between US and multinational forces to coordinate and deconflict airspace requirements.

j. Plans to provide for continuity of airspace control operations under degraded conditions (alternate HQ, alternatives for key radar or C2 nodes, and other required capabilities).

k. Description of the AOD mission and airspace priorities.

l. Description of ACMs and procedures for the joint force.

m. Description of the procedures to propose, approve, modify, and promulgate each procedural ACM available for use within the operational area (i.e., HIDACZ, JEZ, FEZ, MEZ, MRR, CA, air refueling tracks, corridors, ROZs, and other appropriate procedures).

n. Description of IFF/SIF procedures.

o. Description of orbit procedures with retrograde plans.

p. Description of procedures and systems to compile and promulgate the ACO that provides airspace control procedures and/or guidance in effect for a specified time period. The ACO would normally contain:

(1) Modifications to guidance and/or procedures contained in the ACP.

(2) Active or current IFF/SIF procedures.

(3) Location and procedures associated with active procedural ACMs (HIDACZ, JEZ, FEZ, MEZ, MRR, CA, corridors, ROZs, and other appropriate procedures).

(4) Procedures for entering and transiting active ROZs (e.g., AOA).

(5) Location of active orbit areas.

(6) Active UA launch, recovery, and mission areas.

(7) Launch and impact ROZs for surface-to-surface missiles.

(8) FSCMs, both restrictive and permissive (e.g., FSCLs, no-fire areas, restrictive-fire areas, free-fire areas).

(9) Applicable ground force control measures (e.g., battle positions, engagement areas, air axes of advance).

q. Description of the interface with agencies/commands providing intertheater air mobility support for the purpose of coordinating and distributing airspace control information/procedures.

APPENDIX B
AIRSPACE COORDINATING AND FIRE SUPPORT
COORDINATION MEASURES

United States message text format (USMTF) organizes ACMs into a set of broad categories called TYPES. Each type includes a subset of control measures called USAGES. The USMTF TYPES: air defense area, air defense operations area, air traffic control (ATC), air corridor/route, procedural control, reference point, restricted operations zone (ROZ), special use airspace.

Intentionally Blank

ANNEX A TO APPENDIX B
AIRSPACE COORDINATING MEASURE REQUEST
REPRESENTATIVE FORMAT

TO:

FROM:

SUBJECT: Request for Airspace

    (A) Airspace Coordinating Measure Requested

    (B) Location (Latitude/Longitude)

    (C) Altitude(s)

    (D) Valid/Void Times (normally ZULU)

    (E) Type Aircraft/Mission

    (F) Controlling Agency

    (G) Comments

NOTE: This format is representative of the appropriate USMTF. Refer to Military Standard (MIL-STD)-6040, *US Message Text Formatting Program,* and associated directives for detailed instructions.

Intentionally Blank

ANNEX B TO APPENDIX B
AIRSPACE COORDINATING AND FIRE SUPPORT COORDINATION
MEASURES

1. Definitions

The definition and descriptions of airspace coordinating and fire support coordination measures are presented in Figure B-B-1. ACMs are measures employed to facilitate the efficient use of airspace to accomplish missions and simultaneously provide safeguards for friendly forces. ACMs are organized into a set of broad categories called TYPES. Each type includes a subset of control measures called USAGES. The ACM TYPES (with United States Message Test Format [USMTF] abbreviations and number of associated usages) are:

a. Air Defense Area (ADAREA). An area and the airspace above it within procedures are established to minimize mutual interference between air and ground based/Army air defense and other operations.

b. Air Defense Operations Area (ADOA). An area and airspace above it within which procedures are established to minimize mutual interference between maritime and amphibious air defense operations.

c. Air Traffic Control (ATC). Airspace of defined dimension within which air traffic control service is provided to IFR and VFR flights in accordance with civil air traffic control regulations.

d. Air Corridor/Route (CORRTE). A bi-directional or restricted air route of travel specified for use by aircraft.

e. Procedural Control (PROC). An airspace coordinating measure that defines airspace dimensions for enabling other systems (e.g., fire support systems) to discriminate: friendly coordination joint engagement measures from enemy, employ fires across boundaries, coordinate joint engagement of targets for a particular operation, or to delineate an airspace boundary.

f. Reference Point (REFPT). A point or set of coordinates generally used for control purposes or to indicate a reference position.

g. Restricted Operations Zone (ROZ). Airspace reserved for specific activities in which the operation of one or more airspace uses is restricted.

h. Special Use Airspace (SUA). Airspace defined for a specific purpose; or to designate airspace in which no flight activity is organized.

2. Figure

AIRSPACE AND FIRE SUPPORT COORDINATION MEASURES	
AIR DEFENSE AREA (ADAREA) **(Mapped Usages)**	
Air Defense Identification Zone	ADIZ
Base Defense Zone	BDZ
Buffer Zone	BZ
High-Altitude Missile Engagement Zone	HIMEZ
High-Density Airspace Control Zone	HIDACZ
Joint Engagement Zone	JEZ
Joint Operations Area	JOA
Land Fighter Engagement Zone (LFEZ is the USTMF used for Fighter Engagement Zone [FEZ])	LFEZ
Land Missile Engagement Zone	LMEZ
Low-Altitude Missile Engagement Zone	LOMEZ
Short-Range Air Defense Engagement Zone	SHORAD
Weapons Free Zone	WFZ
AIR DEFENSE OPERATIONS AREA (ADOA) **(Mapped Usages)**	
Air Defense Action Area	ADAA
Amphibious Defense Zone	ADZ
Amphibious Objective Area	AOA
Approach Corridor	APPCOR
Battlefield Coordination Line	BCL
Coordinated Air Defense Area	CADA
Carrier Control Zone	CCZONE
Crossover Zone	COZ
Fleet Air Defense Identification Zone (USMTF positive identification radar advisory zone [PIRAZ])	FADIZ
Fire-Power Umbrella	FIRUB
Identification Safety Range	ISR
Maritime Fighter Engagement Zone	MFEZ
Missile Arc	MISARC
Maritime Missile Engagement Zone	MMEZ
Return to Force	RTF
Safe Sector (USMTF Safety Sector)	SAFES
Ship Control Zone	SCZ
AIR TRAFFIC CONTROL (ATC) **(Mapped Usages)**	
Advisory Route	ADVRTE
Airway	ARWY
Air Traffic Service Route	ATSRTE
Conditional Route	CDR

Figure B-B-1. Airspace and Fire Support Coordinating Measures

Class-A Airspace	CLSA
Class-B Airspace	CLSB
Class-C Airspace	CLSC
Class-D Airspace	CLSD
Class-E Airspace	CLSE
Class-F Airspace	CLSF
Class-G Airspace	CLSG
Control Zone	CONTZN
Cross Border Area	CBA (NATO)
Control Area	CTA
Danger Area	DA
Flight Information Region	FIR
Area Navigation Route	NAVRTE
Prohibited Area	PROHIB
Reduced Coordination Area	RCA (NATO)
Restricted Area	RA
Temporary Segregated Area	TSA
Terminal Control Area	TCA
Terminal Radar Service Area	TRSA
Warning Area	WARN
AIR CORRIDOR/ROUTE (CORRTE) **(Mapped Usages)**	
Air Corridor	AIRCOR
Air Route	AIRRTE
Minimum Risk Route	MRR
Standard Use Army Aircraft Flight Route	SAAFR
Special Corridor	SC
Safe Lane	SL
Transit Corridor	TC
Temporary Minimum Risk Route	TMRR
Transit Route	TR
PROCEDURAL CONTROL (PROC) **(Mapped Usages)**	
Airspace Coordination Area	ACA
Altitude Reservation	ALTRV
Boundary	BNDRY
Coordinated Fire Line	CFL
Coordinating Altitude (USMTF uses Coordination Level)	CA (CL)
Forward Edge of the Battle Area	FEBA
Free Fire Area	FFA
Forward Line of Own Troops	FLOT
Fire Support Coordination Line	FSCL

Figure B-B-1. Airspace and Fire Support Coordinating Measures

Identification, Friend or Foe (IFF) Switch Off Line	IFFOFF
IFF Switch On Line	IFFON
Restrictive Fire Area	RFA
Restrictive Fire Line	RFL
Safe Area for Evasion	SAFE
Traverse Level	TL
REFERENCE POINT (REFPT) **(Mapped Usages)**	
Air Control Point	ACP
Bulls-Eye	BULL
Contact Point	CP
Entry/Exit Gate	EG
Hand Over Gate	HG
Identification Safety Point	ISP
Marshalling Gate	MG
Search and Rescue Point	SARDOT
RESTRICTED OPERATIONS ZONE (ROZ) **(Mapped Usages)**	
Air-to-Air Refueling Area	AAR
Airborne Command and Control Area	ABC
Airborne Early Warning Area	AEW
Combat Air Patrol	CAP
Close Air Support Holding Area	CAS
Drop Zone	DZ
Electronic Combat	EC
Landing Zone	LZ
Pickup Zone	PZ
Reconnaissance Area	RECCE
Restricted Operations Area	ROA
Special Electronic Mission Area	SEMA
Special Operations Forces (USMTF used for joint special operations area [JSOA])	SOF
Training Area	TRNG
Unmanned Aircraft (USMTF uses UAV [unmanned aerial vehicle])	UA
SPECIAL USE AIRSPACE (SUA) **(Mapped Usages)**	
Airspace Control Subarea/Sector	ACSS
Alert Area	ALERTA
Airspace Control Area	ASCA
Force Air Coordination Area	FACA
Forward Arming and Refueling Point	FARP
Kill Box	KILLB
Military Operations Area	MOA

Figure B-B-1. Airspace and Fire Support Coordinating Measures

No Fly Area	NOFLY
No Fire Area	NFA
Surface-to-Surface Missile System	SSMS

COORDINATING MEASURE	DEFINITION/ DESCRIPTION	USES/PLANNING CONSIDERATIONS
Advisory Route (ADVRTE)	A designated route along which air traffic advisory service is available	
Air-to-Air Refueling Area (AAR)	Airspace of defined dimensions set aside for air-to-air refueling operations.	AAR tracks are typically set up in a race track configuration.
Airborne Command and Control Area (ABC)	Airspace of defined dimensions established specifically for aircraft conducting battlefield command and control.	
Airborne Early Warning Area (AEW)	Airspace of defined dimensions established specifically for aircraft conducting early warning.	
Air Control Point (ACP)	A point that is defined and used for navigation, command and control, and communication.	Unmanned aircraft system (UAS) routing is normally accomplished through existing air control points.
Air Corridor (AIRCOR)	A restricted air route of travel specified for use by friendly aircraft and established for the purpose of preventing friendly aircraft from being fired on by friendly forces.	Air corridor procedures are used to route aviation combat elements between such areas as forward arming and refueling points, holding areas, and battle positions. Altitudes of and air corridor do not exceed the coordinating altitude, if established. If a coordinating altitude has been established, an air corridor is implemented by the using authority. If a coordinating altitude has not been established, an air corridor is established by the airspace control authority (ACA) at the request of the appropriate ground commander.
Air Defense Action Area (ADAA)	An area and the airspace above it within which friendly aircraft or surface-to-air weapons are normally given precedence in operations except under specified conditions.	An ADAA is used for preference of a specific weapon system over another without excluding the other from use under certain operational conditions. From an airspace control

Figure B-B-1. Airspace and Fire Support Coordinating Measures

COORDINATING MEASURE	DEFINITION/ DESCRIPTION	USES/PLANNING CONSIDERATIONS
		perspective, it provides airspace users with the location of air defense areas for mission planning purposes.
Air Defense Identification Zone (ADIZ)	Airspace of defined dimensions within which the ready identification, location, and control of airborne vehicles are required.	Associated with nations or areas of operation, the ADIZ is normally the transition between procedural control areas (outside) and the positive control areas (inside). Typically, ADIZ is used for sovereign national boundaries, or in the case of areas of operations, for identification in the rear areas.

See flight information publications/International Civil Aviation Organization for theater-specific ADIZ and associated procedures and limitations. |
| Airspace Control Area (ASCA) | Airspace that is laterally defined by the boundaries of the area of operations. The airspace control area may be subdivided into airspace control subareas. (AAP-6) | Airspace control areas are a means of planning or dividing responsibility.

Geographically defined, an airspace control area may include political boundaries. |
| Air Route (AIRRTE) | The navigable airspace between two points, identified to the extent necessary for the application of flight rules. | Established to route nonoperational and operational support traffic through air defenses. |
| Airspace Control Subarea/Sector (ACSS) | A subelement of the airspace control area, established to facilitate the control of the overall area. Airspace control sector boundaries normally coincide with air defense organization subdivision boundaries. Airspace control sectors are designated in accordance with procedures and guidance contained in the airspace control plan in consideration of Service component, host-nation, and multinational airspace control capabilities and | An airspace control sector provides airspace control of an area by a component or other airspace control-capable entity best able to provide control in that geographic area.

An airspace control sector interface with the airspace control system needs to be developed.

Airspace control sectors are designated by the ACA in consideration of joint force component, host-nation, and multinational airspace control capabilities and requirements. |

Figure B-B-1. Airspace and Fire Support Coordinating Measures

COORDINATING MEASURE	DEFINITION/ DESCRIPTION	USES/PLANNING CONSIDERATIONS
	requirements.	
Airspace Coordination Area (ACA)	A three-dimensional block of airspace in a target area, established by the appropriate ground commander, in which friendly aircraft are reasonably safe from friendly surface fires. The airspace coordination area may be formal or informal.	An airspace coordination area is used primarily in close air support situations for high-volume fire. Friendly aircraft are reasonably free from friendly surface fires, with artillery, helicopters, and fixed-winged aircraft given specific lateral or vertical airspace within which to operate.

Timely implementation of the area is dependent on the ground situation. Burden of deconfliction rests with the ground commander.

It is established by the appropriate ground commander. |
Air Traffic Service Route (ATSRTE)	A specified route designed for channeling the flow of traffic as necessary for the provision of air traffic services.	
Airway (ARWY)	A control area or portion thereof established in the form of a corridor equipped with radio navigational aids.	
Alert Area (ALERTA)	Airspace that may contain a high volume of pilot training activities or an unusual type of aerial activity, neither of which is hazardous to aircraft.	
Altitude Reservation (ALTRV)	A block of altitude reserved for aircraft to transit or loiter.	
Amphibious Defense Zone (ADZ)	An area encompassing the amphibious objective area and adjoining airspace as required for the accompanying naval forces for the purpose of air defense.	An ADZ provides an anti-air warfare area for protection of the amphibious task force. If an amphibious defense zone overlaps other land-based air defense areas, appropriate coordination for division of responsibilities and boundaries must be conducted.
Amphibious Objective Area (AOA)	A geographical area (delineated for command and control purposes in the initiating directive) within	It allows the Commander, Amphibious Task Force, freedom of air operations within the AOA.

Figure B-B-1. Airspace and Fire Support Coordinating Measures

COORDINATING MEASURE	DEFINITION/ DESCRIPTION	USES/PLANNING CONSIDERATIONS
	which is located the objective(s) to be secured by the amphibious force. This area must be of sufficient size to ensure accomplishment of the amphibious force's mission and must provide sufficient area for conducting necessary sea, air, and land operations.	Coordination with nonorganic aircraft for entry into and exit from the AOA, and deconfliction within the AOA with operations just outside the AOA normally requires the continuous, active involvement of the affected commanders and staffs.
Approach Corridor (APPCOR)	Airspace established for the safe passage of land-based aircraft joining or departing a maritime force.	
Area Navigation Route (NAVRTE)	An air traffic services route established for the use of aircraft capable of employing area navigation.	
Base Defense Zone (BDZ)	An air defense zone established around an air base and limited to the engagement envelope of short-range air defense weapons systems defending that base. Base defense zones have specific entry, exit, and identification, friend or foe, procedures established.

A zone established around airbases to enhance the effectiveness of local ground-based air defense systems. | A BDZ provides airspace users with location of the engagement zone for the air defense systems defending a base for mission planning purposes. |
| Battlefield Coordination Line (BCL) | A supplementary measure, which facilitates the expeditious attack of surface targets of opportunity between the measure (the BCL) and the fire support coordination line. | |
| Boundary (BNDRY) | A line that delineates surface areas for the purpose of facilitating coordination and deconfliction of operations between adjacent units, formations, or areas.

In land warfare, a line by | |

Figure B-B-1. Airspace and Fire Support Coordinating Measures

COORDINATING MEASURE	DEFINITION/ DESCRIPTION	USES/PLANNING CONSIDERATIONS
	which areas of responsibility between adjacent units and/or formations are defined (AAP-6).	
Buffer Zone (BZ)	Airspace designed specifically to provide a buffer between various airspace coordinating measures.	
Bulls-Eye (BULL)	An established reference point from which the position of an object can be referenced.	
Carrier Control Zone (CCZONE)	The airspace within a circular limit defined by 5 miles horizontal radius from the carrier, extending upward from the surface to and including 2,500 feet unless otherwise designated for special operations, and is under the cognizance of the air officer during visual meteorological conditions.	
Class-A Airspace (CLSA)	Generally, airspace from 18,000 feet mean sea level (MSL) up to and including flight level 600, including airspace overlying the waters within 12 nautical miles of the contiguous states and Alaska. Visual Flight Rules (VFR) operations are not permitted in Class A airspace.	This definition is based on classification of airspace within the US. Airspace classification may vary by specific location. Airmen and airspace planners should refer to the appropriate flight information publication (FLIP) and notices to airmen (NOTAMs), etc., for detailed information and international airspace requirements.
Class-B Airspace (CLSB)	Generally, airspace from the surface to 10,000 feet MSL surrounding the nation's busiest airports in terms of airport operations or passenger enplanements. ATC provides separation between all aircraft inside Class B airspace.	This definition is based on classification of airspace within the US. Airspace classification may vary by specific location. Airmen and airspace planners should refer to the appropriate FLIP and NOTAMs, etc., for detailed information and international airspace requirements.
Class-C Airspace (CLSC)	Generally, airspace from the surface to 4,000 feet above the airport elevation (charted in MSL) surrounding those airports that have an operational control tower,	This definition is based on classification of airspace within the US. Airspace classification may vary by specific location. Airmen and airspace planners should refer to the appropriate

Figure B-B-1. Airspace and Fire Support Coordinating Measures

COORDINATING MEASURE	DEFINITION/ DESCRIPTION	USES/PLANNING CONSIDERATIONS
	are serviced by radar approach control, and have a certain number of instrument flight rules (IFR) operations or passenger enplanements. ATC provides separation between VFR and IFR inside Class C airspace.	FLIP and NOTAMs, etc., for detailed information and international airspace requirements.
Class-D Airspace (CLSD)	Generally, airspace from the surface to 2,500 feet above the airport elevation (charted in MSL) surrounding those airports that have an operational control tower. The configuration of each Class D airspace is individually tailored and when instrument procedures are published, the airspace will normally be designated to contain the procedures. Prior to entering Class D airspace, two-way radio communication must be established and maintained with the ATC facility providing air traffic service.	This definition is based on classification of airspace within the US. Airspace classification may vary by specific location. Airmen and airspace planners should refer to the appropriate FLIP and NOTAMs, etc., for detailed information and international airspace requirements.
Class-E Airspace (CLSE)	Generally, if the airspace is not Class A, B, C, or D, and it is controlled airspace, it is Class E airspace. Also includes federal airways.	This definition is based on classification of airspace within the US. Airspace classification may vary by specific location. Airmen and airspace planners should refer to the appropriate FLIP and NOTAMs, etc., for detailed information and international airspace requirements.
Class-F Airspace (CLSF)	Airspace in which instrument flight rules (IFR) and visual flight rules flights are permitted; all participating IFR flights receive an air traffic advisory service, and all flights receive flight information service if requested.	This classification of airspace is not used within the US (FAAO JO 7400.9T). Airspace classification may vary by specific location. Airmen and airspace planners should refer to the appropriate FLIP and NOTAMs, etc., for detailed information and international airspace requirements.
Class-G Airspace (CLSG)	Airspace not assigned as A, B, C, D, or E is uncontrolled airspace and is designated as Class G airspace.	This definition is based on classification of airspace within the US. Airspace classification may vary by specific location.

Figure B-B-1. Airspace and Fire Support Coordinating Measures

COORDINATING MEASURE	DEFINITION/ DESCRIPTION	USES/PLANNING CONSIDERATIONS
		Airmen and airspace planners should refer to the appropriate FLIP and NOTAMs, etc., for detailed information and international airspace requirements.
Close Air Support Holding Area (CAS)	Airspace designated for holding orbits and used by rotary-and fixed-wing aircraft that are in close proximity to friendly forces.	
Combat Air Patrol (CAP)	An aircraft patrol provided over an objective area, the force protected, the critical area of a combat zone, or in an air defense area, for the purpose of intercepting and destroying hostile aircraft before they reach their targets.	An anti-air warfare activity conducted in support of air operations.
Conditional Route (CDR)	A non-permanent air traffic service route or portion thereof that can be planned and used only under certain conditions.	
Contact Point (CP)	In air operations, the position at which a mission leader makes radio contact with an air control agency.	
Control Area (CTA)	A controlled airspace extending upward from a specified limit above the Earth. (AAP-6)	
Control Zone (CONTZN)	A controlled airspace extending upward from the surface of the Earth to a specified upper limit. (AAP-6)	
Coordinated Air Defense Area (CADA)	A mutually defined block of airspace between a land-based air commander and a naval commander when their forces are operating in close proximity to one another. (AJP-3.3.5)	
Coordinated Fire Line (CFL)	A line beyond which conventional and indirect surface fire support means may fire at any time within the boundaries of the establishing headquarters	

Figure B-B-1. Airspace and Fire Support Coordinating Measures

COORDINATING MEASURE	DEFINITION/ DESCRIPTION	USES/PLANNING CONSIDERATIONS
	without additional coordination. The purpose of the coordinated fire line is to expedite the surface-to-surface attack of targets beyond the coordinated fire line without coordination with the ground commander in whose area the targets are located. A line beyond which conventional or improved indirect fire means, such as mortars, field artillery, and naval surface fire may fire without additional coordination. (AJP-3.3.5)	
Coordinating Altitude (CA)	An airspace coordinating measure that uses altitude to separate users as the transition between different airspace coordinating entities.	The airspace coordinating entities should be included in the ACP and promulgated in the ACO. Army echelons incorporate ACP guidance and integrate the ACO, AADP, SPINS, and ATO via operations orders. All airspace users should coordinate with the appropriate airspace coordinating entities when transitioning through or firing through the coordinating altitude.
Coordination Level (CL)	A procedural method to separate fixed- and rotary-wing aircraft by determining an altitude below which fixed-wing aircraft normally will not fly.	
Cross Border Area (CBA) (NATO)	A temporary segregated area established over international boundaries for specific operational requirements.	
Crossover Zone (COZ)	Airspace beyond the missile engagement zone into which fighters may pursue targets to complete interception.	
Danger Area (DA)	In air traffic control, an airspace of defined dimensions within which activities dangerous to the	

Figure B-B-1. Airspace and Fire Support Coordinating Measures

COORDINATING MEASURE	DEFINITION/ DESCRIPTION	USES/PLANNING CONSIDERATIONS
	flight of aircraft may exist at specified times.	
Drop Zone (DZ)	A specific area upon which airborne troops, equipment, or supplies are airdropped.	
Electronic Combat (EC)	Airspace established specifically for aircraft engaging in electronic combat.	
Entry/Exit Gate (EG)	The point to which an aircraft will be directed to commence the transit inbound/outbound from an airfield or force at sea.	
Fighter Engagement Zone (FEZ) (USMTF Land Fighter Engagement Zone [LFEZ])	In air defense, that airspace of defined dimensions within which the responsibility for engagement of air threats normally rests with fighter aircraft. NOTE: To ensure the operational utility of a FEZ, input a LFEZ into a USMTF system. USMTF does not recognize the term FEZ.	These operations usually take place in airspace above and beyond the engagement ranges of surface-based (land and sea), short-range air defense systems, and are an alternative type of engagement operation if the detailed control aspects of joint engagement operations cannot be met. A FEZ normally is used when fighter aircraft have the clear operational advantage over surface-based systems. These advantages could include range, density of fire, rules of engagement, or coordination requirements. From an airspace control perspective, it provides airspace users with location of the engagement zone for fighter aircraft for mission planning purposes. Coordination and flexibility within the combat airspace control system may be a limiting factor. Under FEZ operations, surface-to-air missile systems will not be allowed to fire weapons unless targets are positively identified as hostile and assigned by higher authority, or unless they are firing in self defense.
Fire-Power Umbrella	An area of specified	

Figure B-B-1. Airspace and Fire Support Coordinating Measures

COORDINATING MEASURE	DEFINITION/ DESCRIPTION	USES/PLANNING CONSIDERATIONS
(FIRUB)	dimensions defining the boundaries of the airspace over a naval force at sea within which the fire of ships' anti-aircraft weapons can endanger aircraft, and within which special procedures have been established for the identification and operation of friendly aircraft.	
Fire Support Coordination Line (FSCL)	A fire support coordination measure that is established and adjusted by appropriate land or amphibious force commanders within their boundaries in consultation with superior, subordinate, supporting, and affected commanders. Fire support coordination lines facilitate the expeditious attack of surface targets of opportunity beyond the coordinating measure. A fire support coordination line does not divide an area of operations by defining a boundary between close and deep operations or a zone for close air support. The fire support coordination line applies to all fires of air, land, and sea-based weapon systems using any type of ammunition. Forces attacking targets beyond a fire support coordination line must inform all affected commanders in sufficient time to allow necessary reaction to avoid fratricide. Supporting elements attacking targets beyond the fire support coordination line must ensure that the attack will not produce adverse effects on, or to the rear of, the line. Short of a fire support coordination line, all air-to-ground and surface-to-surface attack operations are controlled by the appropriate land or	

Figure B-B-1. Airspace and Fire Support Coordinating Measures

COORDINATING MEASURE	DEFINITION/ DESCRIPTION	USES/PLANNING CONSIDERATIONS
	amphibious force commander. The fire support coordination line should follow well-defined terrain features. Coordination of attacks beyond the fire support coordination line is especially critical to commanders of air, land, and special operations forces. In exceptional circumstances, the inability to conduct this coordination will not preclude the attack of targets beyond the fire support coordination line. However, failure to do so may increase the risk of fratricide and could waste limited resources. Within an assigned area of operations, a line established by a land or amphibious force commander to denote coordination requirements for fires by other force elements that may affect the commander's current and planned operations. The fire support coordination line applies to fires of air, ground, or sea weapons using any type of ammunition against surface or ground targets. The establishment of the fire support coordination line must be coordinated with the appropriate commanders and supporting elements. Attacks against surface or ground targets short of the fire support coordination line must be conducted under the positive control or procedural clearance of the associated land or amphibious force commander. Unless in exceptional circumstances,	

Figure B-B-1. Airspace and Fire Support Coordinating Measures

COORDINATING MEASURE	DEFINITION/ DESCRIPTION	USES/PLANNING CONSIDERATIONS
	commanders of forces attacking targets beyond the fire support coordination line must coordinate with all affected commanders in order to avoid fratricide and to harmonize joint objectives. Note: In the context of this definition the term "surface targets" applies to those in littoral or inland waters within the designated area of operations. (AAP-6) Boundary used to coordinate fires of air, ground, or sea weapon systems against surface targets. (AJP-3.3.5)	
Fleet Air Defense Identification Zone (FADIZ) (USMTF refers to this as a positive identification radar advisory zone [PIRAZ])	A specified area established for identification and flight following of aircraft in the vicinity of a fleet-defended area.	A FADIZ provides tracking, control, and assistance to friendly aircraft within the antiair of the battle group.
Flight Information Region (FIR)	An airspace of defined dimensions within which flight information service and alerting service are provided.	
Forward Arming and Refueling Point (FARP)	A temporary facility — organized, equipped, and deployed by an aviation commander, and normally located in the main battle area closer to the area where operations are being conducted than the aviation unit's combat service area — to provide fuel and ammunition necessary for the employment of aviation maneuver units in combat. The forward arming and refueling point permits combat aircraft to rapidly refuel and rearm simultaneously.	
Forward Edge of the Battle Area (FEBA)	The foremost limits of a series of areas in which ground combat units are deployed, excluding the	

Figure B-B-1. Airspace and Fire Support Coordinating Measures

COORDINATING MEASURE	DEFINITION/ DESCRIPTION	USES/PLANNING CONSIDERATIONS
	areas in which the covering or screening forces are operating, designed to coordinate fire support, the positioning of forces, or the maneuver of units.	
Forward Line of Own Troops (FLOT)	A line that indicates the most forward positions of friendly forces in any kind of military operation at a specific time. The forward line of own troops normally identifies the forward location covering screening forces. The forward line of own troops may be at, beyond, or short of the forward edge of the battle area. An enemy forward line of own troops indicates the forward-most position of hostile forces. A line that indicates the most forward positions of friendly forces in any kind of military operation at a specific time. (AAP-6)	
Free Fire Area (FFA)	A specific area into which any weapon system may fire without additional coordination with the establishing headquarters.	
Hand-Over Gate (HG)	The point at which the control of the aircraft, if radar hand-over is used, changes from one controller to another.	
High-Altitude Missile Engagement Zone (HIMEZ)	In air defense, that airspace of defined dimensions within which the responsibility for engagement of air threats normally rests with high-altitude surface-to-air missiles.	HIMEZ normally is used when a high-altitude missile system has a clear operational advantage over using aircraft. These advantages could include range, command and control, rules of engagement, or response time. It provides airspace users with location of the engagement zone of a high-altitude missile system for mission planning purposes. Design of the HIMEZ is contingent on specific weapon

Figure B-B-1. Airspace and Fire Support Coordinating Measures

COORDINATING MEASURE	DEFINITION/ DESCRIPTION	USES/PLANNING CONSIDERATIONS
		system capabilities.
High-Density Airspace Control Zone (HIDACZ)	Airspace designated in an airspace control plan or airspace control order, in which there is a concentrated employment of numerous and varied weapons and airspace users. A high density airspace control zone has defined dimensions, which usually coincide with geographical features of navigational aids. Access to a high density airspace control zone is normally controlled by the maneuver commander. The maneuver commander can also direct a more restrictive weapons status within the high density airspace control zone. Airspace of defined dimensions, designated by the airspace control authority, in which there is a concentrated employment of numerous and varied weapons/airspace users. (AAP-6)	HIDACZ allows ground/Marine air-ground task force commanders to restrict a volume of airspace from users not involved with ongoing operations. It restricts use of the airspace because of the large volume and density of fires supporting the fround operations within the described geographic area. The volume of air traffic demands careful coordination to limit the potential conflict among aircraft needed for mission essential operations within the HIDACZ and other airspace users. When establishing a HIDACZ, consider the following: (1) Minimum-risk routes (MRR) into and out of the HIDACZ and to the target area. (2) Air traffic advisory as required. Procedures and systems also must be considered for air traffic control (ATC) service during instrument meteorological conditions. (3) Procedures for expeditious movement of aircraft into and out of the HIDACZ. (4) Coordination of fire support, as well as air defense weapons control orders or status within and in the vicinity of the HIDACZ. (5) Location of enemy forces inside of and within close proximity to the HIDACZ. HIDACZ is nominated by the ground commander and approved by the ACA.

Figure B-B-1. Airspace and Fire Support Coordinating Measures

COORDINATING MEASURE	DEFINITION/ DESCRIPTION	USES/PLANNING CONSIDERATIONS
Identification Safety Point (ISP)	A point at which aircraft, on joining a maritime force, will attempt to establish two-way communications with the surface force and commence identification procedures.	
Identification Safety Range (ISR)	The minimum range to which aircraft may close to a maritime force without having been positively identified as friendly to ensure that the task force/task group does not mistake the aircraft for hostile.	
Identification, Friend or Foe (IFF) Switch Off Line (IFFOFF)	The line demarking where friendly aircraft stop emitting an IFF signal.	
IFF Switch On Line (IFFON)	The line demarking where friendly aircraft start emitting an IFF signal.	
Joint Engagement Zone (JEZ)	In air defense, that airspace of defined dimensions within which multiple air defense systems (surface-to-air missiles and aircraft) are simultaneously employed to engage air threats.	A JEZ provides airspace user with a location for mission planning purposes. JEZs are highly dependent on correct differentiation between friendly, neutral, and enemy aircraft.
Joint Operations Area (JOA)	Area of land, sea, and airspace, defined by a geographic combatant commander or subordinate unified commander, in which a joint force commander (usually a joint task force commander) conducts military operations to accomplish a specific mission. A temporary area defined by the Supreme Allied Commander Europe, in which a designated joint commander plans and executes a specific mission at the operational level of war. A joint operations area and its defining parameters,	

Figure B-B-1. Airspace and Fire Support Coordinating Measures

COORDINATING MEASURE	DEFINITION/ DESCRIPTION	USES/PLANNING CONSIDERATIONS
	such as time, scope of the mission, and geographical area, are contingency- or mission-specific and are normally associated with combined joint task force operations. (AAP-6)	
Joint Special Operations Area (JSOA)	An area of land, sea, and airspace assigned by a joint force commander to the commander of a joint special operations force to conduct special operations activities. It may be limited in size to accommodate a discrete direct action mission or may be extensive enough to allow a continuing broad range of unconventional warfare operations. NOTE: To obtain the operational utility of a JSOA, input SOF into a USMTF system as USMTF does not recognize JSOA.	
Kill Box (KILLBX)	A kill box is a three-dimensional area used to facilitate the integration of joint fires.	
Landing Zone (LZ)	Any specified zone used for the landing of aircraft.	
Land Missile Engagement Zone (LMEZ)	Airspace of defined dimensions within which responsibility for engagement of air threats normally rests with surface based air defense system.	
Low-Altitude Missile Engagement Zone (LOMEZ)	In air defense, that airspace of defined dimensions within which the responsibility for engagement of air threats normally rests with low-to-medium-altitude surface-to-air missiles.	LOMEZs provide airspace users with the location of the engagement zone of low-altitude missile systems for mission planning purposes. The design of the LOMEZ is contingent on specific weapon system capabilities.
Maritime Fighter Engagement Zone (MFEZ)	The airspace beyond the crossover zone out to limits defined by the officer in	

Figure B-B-1. Airspace and Fire Support Coordinating Measures

COORDINATING MEASURE	DEFINITION/ DESCRIPTION	USES/PLANNING CONSIDERATIONS
	tactical command, in which fighters have freedom of action to identity and engage air targets.	
Maritime Missile Engagement Zone (MMEZ)	A designated airspace in which, under weapons control status "weapons free," ships are automatically cleared to fire at any target which penetrates the zone, unless known to be friendly, adhering to airspace control procedures or unless otherwise directed by the anti-warfare commander.	
Marshalling Gate (MG)	A point to which aircraft fly for air traffic control purposes prior to commencing an outbound transit after takeoff or prior to landing.	
Military Operations Area (MOA)	Airspace designated outside Class A airspace area to separate or segregate certain non-hazardous military from IFR traffic and to identify for visual flight rules (VFR) traffic where these activities are conducted.	
Minimum-Risk Route (MRR)	A temporary corridor of defined dimensions recommended for use by high-speed, fixed-wing aircraft that presents the minimum known hazards to low-flying aircraft transiting the combat zone.	MRRs are used primarily for cross-forward line of own troops operations. Close air support aircraft do not usually use MRRs in the vicinity of the target area. MRRs are established based on known threats.
Missile Arc (MISARC)	An area of 10 degrees or as large as ordered by the officer in tactical command, centered on the bearing of the target with a range that extends to the maximum range of the surface-to-air missile.	
No Fire Area (NFA)	An area designated by the appropriate commander into which fires or their effects are prohibited.	

Figure B-B-1. Airspace and Fire Support Coordinating Measures

COORDINATING MEASURE	DEFINITION/ DESCRIPTION	USES/PLANNING CONSIDERATIONS
No Fly Area (NOFLY)	Airspace of specific dimensions set aside for a specific purpose in which no aircraft operations are permitted, except as authorized by the appropriate commander and controlling agency.	
Pickup Zone (PZ)	Aerial retrieval area.	
Prohibited Area (PROHIB)	A specified area within the land areas of a state or its internal waters, archipelagic waters, or territorial sea adjacent thereto over which the flight of aircraft is prohibited. May also refer to land or sea areas to which access is prohibited.	
Reconnaissance Area (RECCE)	Airspace established specifically for aircraft conducting reconnaissance.	
Reduced Coordination Area (RCA) (NATO)	A portion of defined dimensions within which general air traffic is permitted "off-route" without requiring general air traffic controllers to initiate coordination with operational air traffic controllers.	
Restricted Area (RA)	Restricted area (air) — Designated areas established by appropriate authority over which flight of aircraft is restricted. They are shown on aeronautical charts, published in notices to airmen, and provided in publications of aids to air navigation. An airspace of defined dimensions, above the land areas or territorial waters of a state, within which the flight of aircraft is restricted in accordance with certain specified conditions.	
Restricted Operations Area (ROA)	Airspace of defined dimensions, designated by the airspace control authority, in response to	A ROA is used to separate and identify areas. For example, artillery, mortar, naval surface fire support, UAS operating

Figure B-B-1. Airspace and Fire Support Coordinating Measures

COORDINATING MEASURE	DEFINITION/ DESCRIPTION	USES/PLANNING CONSIDERATIONS
	specific operational situations/requirements within which the operation of one or more airspace users is restricted.	areas, aerial refueling, concentrated interdiction areas, areas of combat search and rescue (CSAR), SOF operating areas, and areas which the area air defense commander (AADC) has declared "weapons free." Commonly used for drop zones, landing zones, SAR areas, UAS launch and recovery sites, UAS mission areas, surface-to-surface missile launch sites, missile flight paths (if necessary), and predicted missile munitions impact locations, and special electronics mission aircraft. ROA can adversely affect air defense operations; therefore, air defense missions generally have priority over ROAs.
Restrictive Fire Area (RFA)	An area in which specific restrictions are imposed and into which fires that exceed those restrictions will not be delivered without coordination with the establishing headquarters.	
Restrictive Fire Line (RFL)	A line established between converging friendly surface forces that prohibits fires or their effects across that line.	
Return to Force (RTF)	Planned route profiles for use by friendly aircraft returning to an aviation-capable ship.	RTF provides a means for easily identifying friendly aircraft.
Safe Area for Evasion (SAFE)	A designated area in hostile territory that offers the evader or escapee a reasonable chance of avoiding capture and of surviving until he can be evacuated.	
Safe Lane (SL)	A bi-directional lane connecting an airbase, landing site, and/or base defense zone to adjacent routes/corridors. Safe lanes	

Figure B-B-1. Airspace and Fire Support Coordinating Measures

COORDINATING MEASURE	DEFINITION/ DESCRIPTION	USES/PLANNING CONSIDERATIONS
	may also be used to connect adjacent activated routes/corridors.	
Safe Sector (USMTF Safety Sector) (SAFES)	Established to route friendly aircraft to maritime forces with minimum risk. (AJP 3.3.5)	
Search and Rescue Point (SARDOT)	A reference point used in search and rescue operations.	
Ship Control Zone (SCZ)	An area activated around a ship operating aircraft, which is not to be entered by friendly aircraft without permission, in order to prevent friendly interference.	
Short-Range Air Defense Engagement Zone (SHORAD)	In air defense, that airspace of defined dimensions within which the responsibility for engagement of air threats normally rests with short-range air defense weapons. It may be established within a low-or high-altitude missile engagement zone.	A short-range air defense engagement zone is normally established for the local air defense of high-value assets. It provides airspace users with the location of the engagement zone of short-range air defense systems for mission planning purposes. Centralized control of a short-range air defense engagement zone may not be possible.
Special Corridor (SC)	An area established to accommodate the special routing requirements of special missions.	
Special Electronic Mission Area (SEMA)	Airspace of defined dimensions established specifically for airborne platforms conducting missions. Generally, it is designed for aircraft such as Compass Call.	
Standard Use Army Aircraft Flight Route (SAAFR)	Route established below the coordinating altitude to facilitate the movement of Army aviation assets. Routes are normally located in the corps through brigade rear areas of operation and do not require approval by the airspace control authority.	SAAFR is an airspace coordinating measure used by Army assets for administrative and logistic purposes. If altitudes are at or below the coordinating altitude, SAAFRs are implemented by the using authority. If a coordinating altitude has not been established, an air corridor is

Figure B-B-1. Airspace and Fire Support Coordinating Measures

COORDINATING MEASURE	DEFINITION/ DESCRIPTION	USES/PLANNING CONSIDERATIONS
		established by the ACA at the request of the appropriate ground commander. See FM 100-10 for additional information.
Surface-to-Surface Missile System (SSMS)	Airspace defined specifically for Army Tactical Missile System and Tomahawk land-attack missile launch and impact points.	
Temporary Minimum Risk Route (TMRR)	A temporary route established to route air traffic between transit routes or the rear boundary of the forward area and their operations area in direct support of ground operations.	
Temporary Segregated Area (TSA)	An airspace of defined dimensions within which activities require the reservation of airspace for the exclusive use of specific users during a determined period of time.	
Terminal Control Area (TCA)	A control area or portion thereof normally situated at the confluence of air traffic service routes in the vicinity of one or more major airfields.	
Terminal Radar Service Area (TRSA)	Airspace surrounding designated airports wherein ATC provides radar vectoring, sequencing, and separation on a full-time basis for all IFR and participating VFR aircraft.	
Training Area (TRNG)	Airspace created during contingency for the purpose of conducting training.	
Transit Corridor (TC)	A bi-directional corridor in the rear area. Air traffic services not normally provided.	Established to route aircraft through air defenses, in the rear area where appropriate, with minimum risk. Pre-planned TCs will be published in ACPs, as will their horizontal and vertical dimensions.

Figure B-B-1. Airspace and Fire Support Coordinating Measures

Transit Route (TR)	In air operations, a temporary air corridor of defined dimensions established in the forward area to minimize the risks to friendly aircraft from friendly air defenses or surface forces.	
Traverse Level (TL)	That vertical displacement above low-level air defense systems, expressed both as a height and an altitude, at which aircraft can cross that area.	TLs normally will be used in conjunction with TCs as specified in ACPs.
Unmanned Aircraft (UA)	Airspace of defined dimensions created specifically for UA operations. Generally, this airspace will consist of the area in which UA missions are conducted, not en route airspace.	
Warning Area (WARN)	Airspace of defined dimensions extending from three nautical miles outward from the coast of the US that contains activity that may be hazardous to nonparticipating aircraft.	
Weapons Free Zone (WFZ)	An air defense zone established for the protection of key assets or facilities, other than air bases, where weapons systems may be fired at any target not positively recognized as friendly.	A weapons free zone is normally used for high-value assets defense and in areas with limited command and control authority. This zone provides airspace users with the location of a weapons free area for mission planning purposes. The AADC declares weapons free with the ACA establishing the zone.

Figure B-B-1. Airspace and Fire Support Coordinating Measures

For the standard formats, contents, and procedures for the US Message Text Format (USMTF) Program, refer to MIL-STD-6040B, DOD Interface Standard, US Message Text Format (USMTF) Description. *The USMTF web site on DKO is URL https://www.us.army.mil/suite/page/441756.*

For detailed ACM and fires systems interoperability, see FM 3-52.1/AFTTP 3-2.78, Multi-Service Tactics, Techniques and Procedures for Airspace Control.

APPENDIX C
REFERENCES

1. **General**

   a. Title 10, US Code.

   b. Federal Aviation Administration Order (FAAO) JO 4200.2G, *Procedures for Handling Airspace Matters.*

   c. FAAO JO 7110.10T, *Flight Services.*

   d. FAAO JO 7400.9T, *Airspace Designations and Reporting Points.*

2. **DOD Publication**

   DOD Directive 5100.1, *Functions of the Department of Defense and Its Major Components.*

3. **Chairman of the Joint Chiefs of Staff (CJCS) Publications**

   a. CJCS Instruction 3151.01A, *Global Command and Control System Common Operational Picture Reporting Requirements.*

   b. CJCS Manual (CJCSM) 3122.01A, *Joint Operation Planning and Execution System (JOPES),Volume I, Planning Policies and Procedures.*

   c. CJCSM 3122.03C, *JOPES, Volume II, Planning Formats.*

   d. JP 1, *Doctrine for the Armed Forces of the United States.*

   e. JP 1-02, *DOD Dictionary of Military and Associated Terms.*

   f. JP 2-0, *Joint Intelligence.*

   g. JP 2-01, *Joint and National Intelligence Support to Military Operations.*

   h. JP 2-01.3, *Joint Intelligence Preparation of the Operational Environment.*

   i. JP 3-0, *Joint Operations.*

   j. JP 3-01, *Countering Air and Missile Threats.*

   k. JP 3-02, *Amphibious Operations.*

   l. JP 3-03, *Joint Interdiction.*

m. JP 3-04, *Joint Shipboard Helicopter Operations.*

n. JP 3-05, *Special Operations.*

o. JP 3-06, *Joint Urban Operations.*

p. JP 3-08, *Interorganizational Coordination During Joint Operations.*

q. JP 3-09, *Joint Fire Support.*

r. JP 3-09.3, *Close Air Support.*

s. JP 3-14, *Space Operations.*

t. JP 3-16, *Multinational Operations.*

u. JP 3-17, *Air Mobility Operations.*

v. JP 3-30, *Command and Control for Joint Air Operations.*

w. JP 3-59, *Meteorological and Oceanographic Operations.*

x. JP 3-60, *Joint Targeting.*

y. JP 4-0, *Joint Logistics.*

z. JP 5-0, *Joint Operation Planning.*

4. **Multi-Service Publication**

a. FM 3-04.15/NTTP 3-55.14/AFTTP(I) 3-2.64, *Multi-Service Tactics, Techniques, and Procedures for the Tactical Employment of Unmanned Aircraft Systems.*

b. FM 3-52.1/AFTTP 3-2.78, *Multi-Service Tactics, Techniques, and Procedures for Airspace Control.*

5. **North Atlantic Treaty Organization (NATO) Publications**

a. Allied Administrative Publication, NATO Dictionary.

b. Allied Joint Publication-3.3.5, *Doctrine for Joint Airspace Control.*

APPENDIX D
ADMINISTRATIVE INSTRUCTIONS

1. User Comments

Users in the field are highly encouraged to submit comments on this publication to: Commander, United States Joint Forces Command, Joint Warfighting Center, ATTN: Joint Doctrine Group, 116 Lake View Parkway, Suffolk, VA 23435-2697. These comments should address content (accuracy, usefulness, consistency, and organization), writing, and appearance.

2. Authorship

The lead agent for this publication is the US Air Force. The Joint Staff doctrine sponsor for this publication is the Director for Operations (J-3).

3. Supersession

This publication supersedes JP 3-52, August 2004, *Doctrine for Joint Airspace Control in the Combat Zone*.

4. Change Recommendations

a. Recommendations for urgent changes to this publication should be submitted:

TO: LEMAY CENTER MAXWELL AFB AL//CC//
INFO: JOINT STAFF WASHINGTON DC//J7-JEDD//
CDR: USJFCOM NORFOLK VA//DOC GP//

Routine changes should be submitted to the Commander, Joint Warfighting Center – Doctrine and Education Group, and info the Director for Operational Plans and Joint Force Development (J-7)/JEDD, via the CJCS JEL at http://www.ditc.mil/doctrine.

b. When a Joint Staff directorate submits a proposal to the CJCS that would change source document information reflected in this publication, that directorate will include a proposed change to this publication as an enclosure to its proposal. The Military Services and other organizations are requested to notify the Joint Staff/J-7 when changes to source documents reflected in this publication are initiated.

c. Record of Changes:

CHANGE NUMBER	COPY NUMBER	DATE OF CHANGE	DATE ENTERED	POSTED BY	REMARKS

5. Distribution of Publications

Local reproduction is authorized and access to unclassified publications is unrestricted. However, access to and reproduction authorization for classified JPs must be in accordance with DOD 5200.1-R, *Information Security Program.*

6. Distribution of Electronic Publications

a. Joint Staff J-7 will not print copies of JPs for distribution. Electronic versions are available on JDEIS at https://jdeis.js.mil (NIPRNET), and https://jdeis.js.smil.mil (SIPRNET) and on the JEL at http://www.dtic.mil/doctrine (NIPRNET).

b. Only approved JPs and joint test publications are releasable outside the combatant commands, Services, and Joint Staff. Release of any classified JP to foreign governments or foreign nationals must be requested through the local embassy (Defense Attaché Office) to DIA Foreign Liaison/IE-3, 200 MacDill Blvd., Bolling AFB, Washington, DC 20340-5100.

c. CD-ROM. Upon request of a JDDC member, the Joint Staff J-7 will produce and deliver one CD-ROM with current JPs.

GLOSSARY
PART I — ABBREVIATIONS AND ACRONYMS

AADC	area air defense commander
AADP	area air defense plan
AAR	air-to-air refueling area
ACA	airspace control authority
ACM	airspace coordinating measure
ACO	airspace control order
ACP	airspace control plan
ACS	airspace control system
AFTTP	Air Force Tactics, Techniques, and Procedures
AFTTP(I)	Air Force Tactics, Techniques, and Procedures (Instruction)
AIP	aeronautical information publication
AO	area of operations
AOA	amphibious objective area
AOD	air operations directive
ATACMS	Army Tactical Missile System
ATC	air traffic control
ATF	amphibious task force
ATO	air tasking order
BDZ	base defense zone
C2	command and control
CA	coordinating altitude
CJCS	Chairman of the Joint Chiefs of Staff
CJCSM	Chairman of the Joint Chiefs of Staff manual
CONOPS	concept of operations
COP	common operational picture
DCA	defensive counterair
DOD	Department of Defense
EW	electronic warfare
FAA	Federal Aviation Administration
FAAO	Federal Aviation Administration order
FEZ	fighter engagement zone
FLOT	forward line of own troops
FM	field manual
FOB	forward operating base
FSCL	fire support coordination line
FSCM	fire support coordination measure
GMLRS	Global Positioning System Multiple Launch Rocket System

HIDACZ	high-density airspace control zone
HN	host nation
HQ	headquarters
IA	information assurance
ICAO	International Civil Aviation Organization
IFF	identification, friend or foe
ISR	intelligence, surveillance, and reconnaissance
JAOP	joint air operations plan
JEZ	joint engagement zone
JFACC	joint force air component commander
JFC	joint force commander
JFLCC	joint force land component commander
JFMCC	joint force maritime component commander
JOA	joint operations area
JOPES	Joint Operation Planning and Execution System
JP	joint publication
LLTR	low-level transit route
MEZ	missile engagement zone
MRR	minimum-risk route
NATO	North Atlantic Treaty Organization
NGO	nongovernmental organization
NOTAM	notice to airmen
NTTP	Navy Tactics, Techniques, and Procedures
OPLAN	operation plan
OPORD	operation order
OPSEC	operations security
ROE	rules of engagement
ROZ	restricted operations zone
SAAFR	standard use Army aircraft flight route
SEAD	suppression of enemy air defenses
SIF	selective identification feature
SOF	special operations forces
SPINS	special instructions
TLAM	Tomahawk land attack missile
TTP	tactics, techniques, and procedures

UA	unmanned aircraft
UAS	unmanned aircraft system
USG	US Government
USMTF	United States message text format

PART II — TERMS AND DEFINITIONS

airborne early warning. The detection of enemy air or surface units by radar or other equipment carried in an airborne vehicle, and the transmitting of a warning to friendly units. Also called AEW. (JP 1-02. SOURCE: JP 3-52)

air corridor. A restricted air route of travel specified for use by friendly aircraft and established for the purpose of preventing friendly aircraft from being fired on by friendly forces. (JP 1-02. SOURCE: JP 3-52)

aircraft control and warning system. None. (Upon approval of this revision, this term and its definition will be removed from JP 1-02.)

aircraft vectoring. None. (Upon approval of this revision, this term and its definition will be removed from JP 1-02.)

air defense. Defensive measures designed to destroy attacking enemy aircraft or missiles in the atmosphere, or to nullify or reduce the effectiveness of such attack. Also called AD. (JP 1-02. SOURCE: JP 3-01)

air defense identification zone. Airspace of defined dimensions within which the ready identification, location, and control of airborne vehicles are required. Also called ADIZ. (JP 1-02. SOURCE: JP 3-52)

air interdiction. Air operations conducted to divert, disrupt, delay, or destroy the enemy's military potential before it can be brought to bear effectively against friendly forces, or to otherwise achieve objectives. Air interdiction is conducted at such distance from friendly forces that detailed integration of each air mission with the fire and movement of friendly forces is not required. (JP 1-02. SOURCE: JP 3-0)

airport surveillance radar. None. (Upon approval of this revision, this term and its definition will be removed from JP 1-02.)

airport traffic area. None. (Upon approval of this revision, this term and its definition will be removed from JP 1-02.)

air route. The navigable airspace between two points, identified to the extent necessary for the application of flight rules. (JP 1-02. SOURCE: JP 3-52)

airspace control. A process used to increase operational effectiveness by promoting the safe, efficient, and flexible use of airspace. (Upon approval of this revision, this term and its definition will modify the existing term and its definition and will be included in JP 1-02.)

airspace control area. Airspace that is laterally defined by the boundaries of the operational area and may be subdivided into airspace control sectors. (JP 1-02. SOURCE: JP 3-01)

airspace control authority. The commander designated to assume overall responsibility for the operation of the airspace control system in the airspace control area. Also called ACA. (JP 1-02. SOURCE: JP 3-52)

airspace control boundary. None. (Upon approval of this revision, this term and its definition will be removed from JP 1-02.)

airspace control center. None. (Upon approval of this publication, this term and its definition will be removed from JP 1-02.)

airspace control facility. None. (Upon approval of this publication, this term and its definition will be removed from JP 1-02.)

airspace control in the combat zone. None. (Upon approval of this publication, this term and its definition will be removed from JP 1-02.)

airspace control order. An order implementing the airspace control plan that provides the details of the approved requests for airspace coordinating measures. It is published either as part of the air tasking order or as a separate document. Also called ACO. (JP 1-02. SOURCE: JP 3-52)

airspace control plan. The document approved by the joint force commander that provides specific planning guidance and procedures for the airspace control system for the joint force operational area. Also called ACP. (JP 1-02. SOURCE: JP 3-52)

airspace control procedures. Rules, mechanisms, and directions that facilitate the control and use of airspace of specified dimensions. (JP 1-02. SOURCE: JP 3-52)

airspace control sector. A subelement of the airspace control area, established to facilitate the control of the overall area. Airspace control sector boundaries normally coincide with air defense organization subdivision boundaries. Airspace control sectors are designated in accordance with procedures and guidance contained in the airspace control plan in consideration of Service component, host nation, and multinational airspace control capabilities and requirements. (JP 1-02. SOURCE: JP 3-52)

airspace control system. An arrangement of those organizations, personnel, policies, procedures, and facilities required to perform airspace control functions. Also called ACS. (JP 1-02. SOURCE: JP 3-52)

airspace coordinating measures. Measures employed to facilitate the efficient use of airspace to accomplish missions and simultaneously provide safeguards for friendly forces. Also called ACMs. (JP 1-02. SOURCE: JP 3-52)

airspace coordination area. A three-dimensional block of airspace in a target area, established by the appropriate ground commander, in which friendly aircraft are reasonably safe from friendly surface fires. The airspace coordination area may be formal or informal. Also called ACA. (JP 1-02. SOURCE: JP 3-09.3)

airspace management. The coordination, integration, and regulation of the use of airspace of defined dimensions. (JP 1-02. SOURCE: JP 3-52)

airspace restrictions. None. (Upon approval of this revision, this term and its definition will be removed from JP 1-02.)

air space warning area. None. (Upon approval of this revision, this term and its definition will be removed from JP 1-02.)

air tasking order. A method used to task and disseminate to components, subordinate units, and command and control agencies projected sorties, capabilities and/or forces to targets and specific missions. Normally provides specific instructions to include call signs, targets, controlling agencies, etc., as well as general instructions. Also called ATO. (JP 1-02. SOURCE: JP 3-30)

air traffic control and landing system. None. (Upon approval of this revision, this term and its definition will be removed from JP 1-02.)

air traffic control center. None. (Upon approval of this revision, this term and its definition will be removed from JP 1-02.)

air traffic control facility. None. (Upon approval of this revision, this term and its definition will be removed from JP 1-02.)

air traffic controller. An air controller specially trained and certified for civilian air traffic control. (JP 1-02. SOURCE: JP 3-52)

air traffic identification. None. (Upon approval of this revision, this term and its definition will be removed from JP 1-02.)

alerting service. A service provided to notify appropriate organizations regarding aircraft in need of search and rescue aid, and assist such organizations as required. (JP 1-02. SOURCE: JP 3-52)

allocation. In a general sense, distribution for employment of limited forces and resources among competing requirements. Specific allocations (e.g., air sorties, nuclear weapons, forces, and transportation) are described as allocation of air sorties, nuclear weapons, etc. (JP 1-02. SOURCE: JP 5-0)

amphibious objective area. A geographical area (delineated for command and control purposes in the initiating directive) within which is located the objective(s) to be secured by the amphibious force. This area must be of sufficient size to ensure accomplishment of the amphibious force's mission and must provide sufficient area for conducting necessary sea, air, and land operations. Also called AOA. (JP 1-02. SOURCE: JP 3-02)

apportionment (air). The determination and assignment of the total expected effort by percentage and/or by priority that should be devoted to the various air operations for a given period of time. Also called air apportionment. (JP 1-02. SOURCE: JP 3-0)

area air defense commander. Within a unified command, subordinate unified command, or joint task force, the commander will assign overall responsibility for air defense to a single commander. Normally, this will be the component commander with the preponderance of air defense capability and the command, control, and communications capability to plan and execute integrated air defense operations. Representation from the other components involved will be provided, as appropriate, to the area air defense commander's headquarters. Also called AADC. (JP 1-02. SOURCE: JP 3-52)

base defense zone. An air defense zone established around an air base and limited to the engagement envelope of short-range air defense weapons systems defending that base. Base defense zones have specific entry, exit, and identification, friend or foe procedures established. Also called BDZ. (JP 1-02. SOURCE: JP 3-10)

carrier control zone. The airspace within a circular limit defined by 5 miles horizontal radius from the carrier, extending upward from the surface to and including 2,500 feet unless otherwise designated for special operations, and is under the cognizance of the air officer during visual meteorological conditions. (Upon approval of this revision, this term and its definition will be included in JP 1-02.)

centralized control. 1. In air defense, the control mode whereby a higher echelon makes direct target assignments to fire units. 2. In joint air operations, placing within one commander the responsibility and authority for planning, directing, and coordinating a military operation or group/category of operations. (JP 1-02. SOURCE: JP 3-30)

collateral damage. Unintentional or incidental injury or damage to persons or objects that would not be lawful military targets in the circumstances ruling at the time. Such damage is not unlawful so long as it is not excessive in light of the overall military advantage anticipated from the attack. (JP 1-02. SOURCE: JP 3-60)

combat airspace control. None. (Upon approval of this publication, this term and its definition will be removed from JP 1-02.)

combat zone. 1. That area required by combat forces for the conduct of operations. 2. The territory forward of the Army rear area boundary. (JP 1-02. SOURCE: JP 3-0)

combined operation. None. (Upon approval of this publication, this term and its definition will be removed from JP 1-02.)

concept of operations. A verbal or graphic statement that clearly and concisely expresses what the joint force commander intends to accomplish and how it will be done using available resources. The concept is designed to give an overall picture of the operation. Also called commander's concept or CONOPS. (JP 1-02. SOURCE: JP 5-0)

controlled airspace. An airspace of defined dimensions within which civilian air traffic control services are provided to control flights. (JP 1-02. SOURCE: JP 3-52)

control zone. A controlled airspace extending upwards from the surface of the Earth to a specified upper limit. (JP 1-02. SOURCE: JP 3-52)

coordinating altitude. An airspace coordinating measure that uses altitude to separate users and as the transition between different airspace coordinating entities. (Upon approval of this revision, this term and its definition will modify the existing term and its definition and will be included in JP 1-02. SOURCE: JP 3-52.)

counterair. A mission that integrates offensive and defensive operations to attain and maintain a desired degree of air superiority. Counterair missions are designed to destroy or negate enemy aircraft and missiles, both before and after launch. (JP 1-02. SOURCE: JP 3-01)

decentralized execution. Delegation of execution authority to subordinate commanders. (JP 1-02. SOURCE: JP 3-30)

defensive counterair. All defensive measures designed to detect, identify, intercept, and destroy or negate enemy forces attempting to penetrate or attack through friendly airspace. Also called DCA. (JP 1-02. SOURCE: JP 3-01)

fighter engagement zone. In air defense, that airspace of defined dimensions within which the responsibility for engagement of air threats normally rests with fighter aircraft. Also called FEZ. (Upon approval of this revision, this term and its definition will modify the existing term and its definition and will be included in JP 1-02.)

fire support coordination. The planning and executing of fire so that targets are adequately covered by a suitable weapon or group of weapons. (JP 1-02. SOURCE: JP 3-09)

fire support coordination measure. A measure employed by land or amphibious commanders to facilitate the rapid engagement of targets and simultaneously provide safeguards for friendly forces. Also called FSCM. (JP 1-02. SOURCE: JP 3-0)

flight information region. An airspace of defined dimensions within which flight information service and alerting service are provided. Also called FIR. (JP 1-02. SOURCE: JP 3-52)

flight information service. A service provided for the purpose of giving advice and information useful for the safe and efficient conduct of flights. Also called FIS. (JP 1-02. SOURCE: JP 3-52)

flight path. None. (Upon approval of this revision, this term and its definition will be removed from JP 1-02.)

flight plan. None. (Upon approval of this revision, this term and its definition will be removed from JP 1-02.)

forward line of own troops. A line that indicates the most forward positions of friendly forces in any kind of military operation at a specific time. The forward line of own troops normally identifies the forward location of covering and screening forces. The forward line of own troops may be at, beyond, or short of the forward edge of the battle area. An enemy forward line of own troops indicates the forward-most position of hostile forces. Also called FLOT. (JP 1-02. SOURCE: JP 3-03)

high-altitude missile engagement zone. In air defense, that airspace of defined dimensions within which the responsibility for engagement of air threats normally rests with high-altitude surface-to-air missiles. Also called HIMEZ. (Upon approval of this revision, this term and its definition will modify the existing term and its definition and will be included in JP 1-02.)

high-density airspace control zone. Airspace designated in an airspace control plan or airspace control order, in which there is a concentrated employment of numerous and varied weapons and airspace users. A high-density airspace control zone has defined dimensions which usually coincide with geographical features or navigational aids. Access to a high-density airspace control zone is normally controlled by the maneuver commander. The maneuver commander can also direct a more restrictive weapons status within the high-density airspace control zone. Also called HIDACZ. (JP 1-02. SOURCE: JP 3-52)

identification, friend or foe. A device that emits a signal positively identifying it as a friendly. Also called IFF. (JP 1-02. SOURCE: 3-52)

identification, friend or foe/selective identification feature procedures. None. (Upon approval of this revision, this term and its definition will be removed from JP 1-02.)

identification maneuver. A maneuver performed for identification purposes. (JP 1-02. SOURCE: JP 3-52)

interdiction. An action to divert, disrupt, delay, or destroy the enemy's military surface capability before it can be used effectively against friendly forces, or to otherwise achieve objectives. (JP 1-02. SOURCE: JP 3-03)

joint air operations. Air operations performed with air capabilities/forces made available by components in support of the joint force commander's operation or campaign objectives, or in support of other components of the joint force. (JP 1-02. SOURCE: JP 3-30)

joint air operations plan. A plan for a connected series of joint air operations to achieve the joint force commander's objectives within a given time and joint operational area. Also called JAOP. (JP 1-02. SOURCE: JP 3-30)

joint engagement zone. In air defense, that airspace of defined dimensions within which multiple air defense systems (surface-to-air missiles and aircraft) are simultaneously employed to engage air threats. Also called JEZ. (Upon approval of this revision, this term and its definition will modify the existing term and its definition and will be included in JP 1-02.)

joint force. A general term applied to a force composed of significant elements, assigned or attached, of two or more Military Departments, operating under a single joint force commander. (JP 1-02. SOURCE: JP 3-0)

joint force air component commander. The commander within a unified command, subordinate unified command, or joint task force responsible to the establishing commander for making recommendations on the proper employment of assigned, attached, and/or made available for tasking air forces; planning and coordinating air operations; or accomplishing such operational missions as may be assigned. The joint force air component commander is given the authority necessary to accomplish missions and tasks assigned by the establishing commander. Also called JFACC. (JP 1-02. SOURCE: JP 3-0)

joint force commander. A general term applied to a combatant commander, subunified commander, or joint task force commander authorized to exercise combatant command (command authority) or operational control over a joint force. Also called JFC. (JP 1-02. SOURCE: JP 1)

joint operations area. An area of land, sea, and airspace, defined by a geographic combatant commander or subordinate unified commander, in which a joint force commander (normally a joint task force commander) conducts military operations to accomplish a specific mission. (JP 1-02. SOURCE: JP 3-0)

low-altitude missile engagement zone. In air defense, that airspace of defined dimensions within which the responsibility for engagement of air threats normally rests with low- to medium-altitude surface-to-air missiles. Also called LOMEZ. (Upon approval of this revision, this term and its definition will modify the existing term and its definition and will be included in JP 1-02.)

low-level transit route. A temporary corridor of defined dimensions established in the forward area to minimize the risk to friendly aircraft from friendly air defenses or surface forces. Also called LLTR. (Upon approval of this revision, this term and its definition will modify the existing term and its definition and will be included in JP 1-02. SOURCE: JP 3-52)

master air attack plan. A plan that contains key information that forms the foundation of the joint air tasking order. Sometimes referred to as the air employment plan or joint air tasking order shell. Information that may be found in the plan includes joint force commander guidance, joint force air component commander guidance, support plans, component requests, target update requests, availability of capabilities and forces, target information from target lists, aircraft allocation, etc. Also called MAAP. (JP 1-02. SOURCE: JP 3-60)

minimum-risk route. A temporary corridor of defined dimensions recommended for use by high-speed, fixed-wing aircraft that presents the minimum known hazards to low-flying aircraft transiting the combat zone. Also called MRR. (JP 1-02. SOURCE: JP 3-52)

multinational operations. A collective term to describe military actions conducted by forces of two or more nations, usually undertaken within the structure of a coalition or alliance. (JP 1-02. SOURCE: JP 3-16)

operational area. An overarching term encompassing more descriptive terms for geographic areas in which military operations are conducted. Operational areas include, but are not limited to, such descriptors as area of responsibility, theater of war, theater of operations, joint operations area, amphibious objective area, joint special operations area, and area of operations. (JP 1-02. SOURCE: JP 3-0)

point defense. The defense or protection of special vital elements and installations; e.g., command and control facilities or air bases. (JP 1-02. SOURCE: JP 3-52)

positive control. A method of airspace control that relies on positive identification, tracking, and direction of aircraft within an airspace, conducted with electronic means by an agency having the authority and responsibility therein. (JP 1-02. SOURCE: JP 3-52)

procedural control. A method of airspace control which relies on a combination of previously agreed and promulgated orders and procedures. (JP 1-02. SOURCE: JP 3-52)

prohibited area. A specified area within the land areas of a state or its internal waters, archipelagic waters, or territorial sea adjacent thereto over which the flight of aircraft is prohibited. May also refer to land or sea areas to which access is prohibited. (JP 1-02. SOURCE: JP 3-52)

radar advisory. The term used to indicate that the provision of advice and information is based on radar observation. (JP 1-02. SOURCE: JP 3-52)

restricted areas (air). Designated areas established by appropriate authority over which flight of aircraft is restricted. They are shown on aeronautical charts, published in notices to airmen, and provided in publications of aids to air navigation. (JP 1-02. SOURCE: JP 3-52)

restricted operations area. Airspace of defined dimensions, designated by the airspace control authority, in response to specific operational situations/requirements within which the operation of one or more airspace users is restricted. Also called ROA. (JP 1-02. SOURCE: JP 3-52)

risk. Probability and severity of loss linked to hazards. (JP 1-02. SOURCE: JP 3-33)

rules of engagement. Directives issued by competent military authority that delineate the circumstances and limitations under which United States forces will initiate and/or continue combat engagement with other forces encountered. Also called ROE. (JP 1-02. SOURCE: JP 1-04)

selective identification feature. A capability that, when added to the basic identification, friend or foe system, provides the means to transmit, receive, and display selected coded replies. (JP 1-02. SOURCE: JP 3-52)

short-range air defense engagement zone. In air defense, that airspace of defined dimensions within which the responsibility for engagement of air threats normally rests with short-range air defense weapons. It may be established within a low- or high-altitude missile engagement zone. Also called SHORADEZ. (Upon approval of this revision, this term and its definition will modify the existing term and its definition and will be included in JP 1-02.)

standard use Army aircraft flight route. Route established below the coordinating altitude to facilitate the movement of Army aviation assets. Route is normally located in the corps through brigade rear areas of operation and do not require approval by the airspace control authority. Also called SAAFR. (Upon approval of this revision, this term and its definition will modify the existing term and its definition and will be included in JP 1-02.)

terminal control area. A control area or portion thereof normally situated at the confluence of air traffic service routes in the vicinity of one or more major airfields. (JP 1-02. SOURCE: JP 3-52)

unmanned aircraft. An aircraft or balloon that does not carry a human operator and is capable of flight under remote control or autonomous programming. Also called UA. (Upon approval of this publication, this term and its definition will be sourced to JP 3-52.)

unmanned aircraft system. That system whose components include the necessary equipment, network, and personnel to control an unmanned aircraft. Also called UAS. (Upon approval of this publication, this term and its definition will be sourced to JP 3-52.)

unmanned aerial vehicle. None. (Upon approval of this publication, this term and its definition will be removed from JP 1-02.)

weapon engagement zone. In air defense, airspace of defined dimensions within which the responsibility for engagement of air threats normally rests with a particular weapon system. Also called WEZ. (Upon approval of this revision, this term and its definition will modify the existing term and its definition and will be included in JP 1-02. SOURCE: JP 3-52.)

weapons free zone. An air defense zone established for the protection of key assets or facilities, other than air bases, where weapon systems may be fired at any target not positively recognized as friendly. (JP 1-02. SOURCE: JP 3-52)

Intentionally Blank

JOINT DOCTRINE PUBLICATIONS HIERARCHY

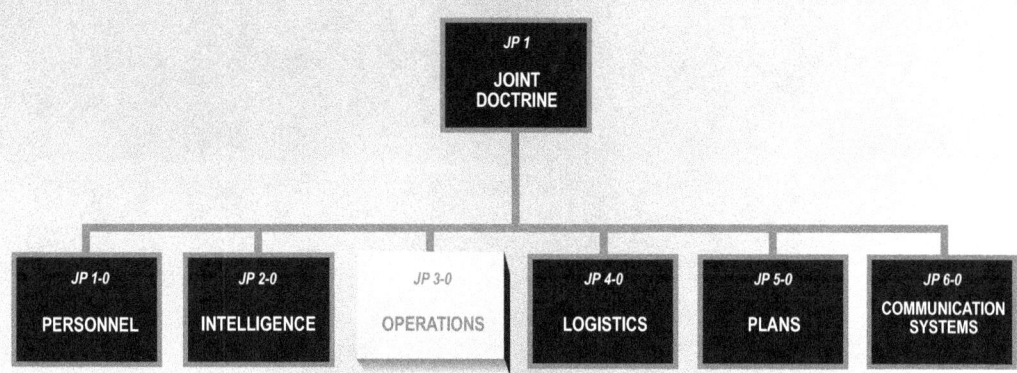

All joint publications are organized into a comprehensive hierarchy as shown in the chart above. **Joint Publication (JP) 3-52** is in the **Operations** series of joint doctrine publications. The diagram below illustrates an overview of the development process:

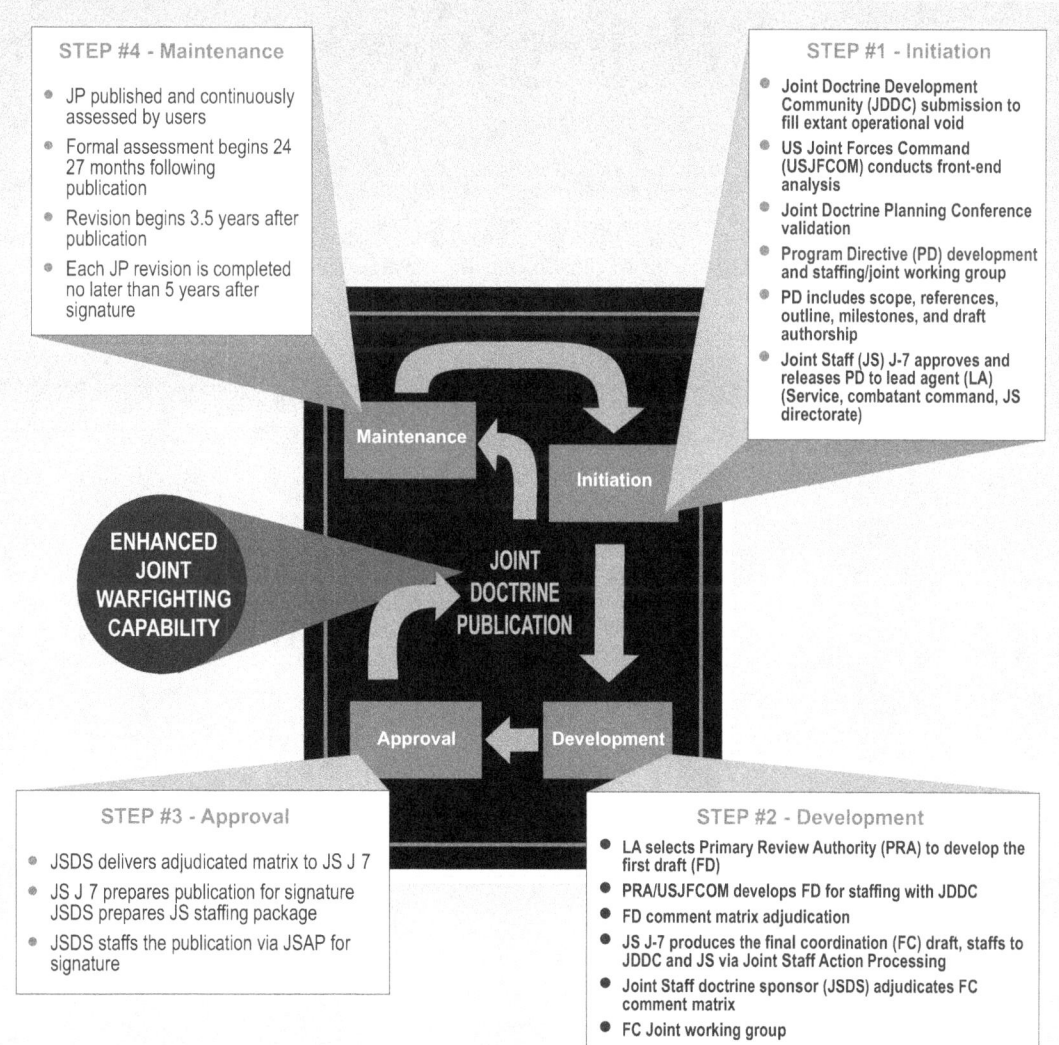

STEP #4 - Maintenance

- JP published and continuously assessed by users
- Formal assessment begins 24 27 months following publication
- Revision begins 3.5 years after publication
- Each JP revision is completed no later than 5 years after signature

STEP #1 - Initiation

- Joint Doctrine Development Community (JDDC) submission to fill extant operational void
- US Joint Forces Command (USJFCOM) conducts front-end analysis
- Joint Doctrine Planning Conference validation
- Program Directive (PD) development and staffing/joint working group
- PD includes scope, references, outline, milestones, and draft authorship
- Joint Staff (JS) J-7 approves and releases PD to lead agent (LA) (Service, combatant command, JS directorate)

STEP #3 - Approval

- JSDS delivers adjudicated matrix to JS J 7
- JS J 7 prepares publication for signature JSDS prepares JS staffing package
- JSDS staffs the publication via JSAP for signature

STEP #2 - Development

- LA selects Primary Review Authority (PRA) to develop the first draft (FD)
- PRA/USJFCOM develops FD for staffing with JDDC
- FD comment matrix adjudication
- JS J-7 produces the final coordination (FC) draft, staffs to JDDC and JS via Joint Staff Action Processing
- Joint Staff doctrine sponsor (JSDS) adjudicates FC comment matrix
- FC Joint working group